EDUCATION IS EVERYBODY'S BUSINESS

A Wake-Up Call to Advocates of Educational Change

Berenice D. Bleedorn

Rowman & Littlefield Education
Lanham, Maryland • Toronto • Oxford
2005

Published in the United States of America
by Rowman & Littlefield Education
A Division of Rowman & Littlefield Publishers, Inc.
A wholly owned subsidiary of The Rowman & Littlefield Publishing Group, Inc.
4501 Forbes Boulevard, Suite 200, Lanham, Maryland 20706
www.rowmaneducation.com

PO Box 317
Oxford
OX2 9RU, UK

British Library Cataloguing in Publication Information Available

Library of Congress Cataloging-in-Publication Data
Bleedorn, Berenice D. Bahr.
  Education is everybody's business : a wake-up call to advocates of
educational change / Berenice D. Bleedorn.
      p. cm.
  Includes bibliographical references and index.
  ISBN 1-57886-298-1 (pbk. : alk. paper)
  1. Creative thinking. 2. Thought and thinking—Study and teaching. 3.
Educational change. I. Title.
  LB1062.B54 2005
  370'.1—dc22

                                                    2005013039

⊗™ The paper used in this publication meets the minimum requirements of
American National Standard for Information Sciences—Permanence of
Paper for Printed Library Materials, ANSI/NISO Z39.48-1992.
Manufactured in the United States of America.

For my daughters, Joan Barnes and Bonnie Sample,
with gratitude for their constant support, appreciation for their
enlightened worldview, and admiration for their dedicated service
to the protection of our natural environment.

CONTENTS

LIST OF FIGURES

FOREWORD

One of the gifts to myself this holiday season was *Exuberance: The Passion for Life*, a new book by Johns Hopkins University psychologist Kay Redfield Jamison that explores the kind of energy important for spurring creative and scientific achievements.

Jamison reminds her readers that "exuberance" is derived from the Latin *exuberance*: *ex* (out of) and *uberare* (to be fruitful, to be abundant). At its core, exuberance is a concept of fertility, or creative production. Reading *Education Is Everybody's Business: A Wake-Up Call to Advocates of Educational Change*, I was struck by how Jamison's descriptions not only described Berenice "Bee" Bleedorn's own journey in the world of creativity but also how extraordinarily well "exuberance" captures the effect that Bleedorn has had on so many others' creativity—including my own. The reader cannot but be engulfed in this exuberance and be motivated to "go out and do likewise."

Education Is Everybody's Business: A Wake-Up Call to Advocates of Educational Change will widen the circle of those who are transformed by Bleedorn's fervent energy for infusing creativity into everyone's educational and learning experiences—and witnessing the impact of these efforts on society, ranging from business to education to democracy to leadership and global concerns.

"Those who are exuberant engage, observe, and respond to the world very differently from those who are not and, what is crucial, they have an intrinsic desire to continue engaging it," writes Jamison. "This engagement is generally not a muted one; rather, it is one filled with a sense of passion, if not actual urgency" (Jamison 2004). The reader cannot miss the urgency and the passion in *Education Is Everybody's Business: A Wake-Up Call to Advocates of Educational Change*. This book is testament to Bleedorn's curiosity and exuberance about the state of the world, the profound impact that creativity can have in making the world better, and the role that education can play in developing individuals who are capable of applying their imagination in a multitude of positive ways.

Bleedorn does indeed engage, observe, and respond to the world very differently—and usually years ahead of many of those around her. Yet she patiently keeps her message alive, while slowly and continually bringing others into her creative worldview. This book blends many of Bleedorn's observations and responses about the world with applications to education, business, and beyond. In chapter 2, "Education: Understand It Backwards, Live It Forwards," the reader will learn how creative thinking and teaching require new approaches, ones that will move the mind and expand one's vision. Looking back at the education system eighty or ninety years ago, Bleedorn gives some profound insights to how learning "happened" then, and demonstrates how those values today offer tactics and strategies to officials with power and authority to design learning processes for citizens in a democracy that enable futuristic thinking. In chapter 3, "The Creativity Factor in Education," she further develops the clarification of the concept of creativity as a fundamental resource worthy of serious study. She shows that knowing the "right answer" is barely the beginning of education and the development of the human mind, and that teaching divergent thinking is essential to the discovery and activation of the human mind.

Bleedorn has never let her passion for creativity burn out—whether it's unlocking her own creativity as a "midlife" college student, developing some of the first creativity and futures college courses in Minnesota, participating in global creativity conferences, or advocating for the importance of creativity in education. Bleedorn embodies the intrinsic desire to continually engage her world, as evident in her nearly fifty years of study and work in the discipline of creativity, most recently reflected in the pages of this book. The topics addressed here bring together the holistic themes that have obsessed Bleedorn's mind throughout her work and teaching. She integrates a diversity of fields necessary for developing and fruitfully applying one's creativity.

Bleedorn writes that the major purpose of this book is "to attract readership among enlightened educators and general public alike so . . . new integrated leadership for enlightened education will emerge." The stories, insights, challenges, and calls to action in the following pages are witness to Bleedorn's own leadership and enlightenment about the interaction between education, creativity, and society. There are few educators today who have been thinking about this issue as long as Bleedorn—and not just thinking but teaching, observing, encouraging, reflecting, and transforming the educational experiences of everyone from children to seniors. Throughout the pages of this book, the reader will see the need to transform education, that transforming education leads to better business and a more peaceful global society.

Creativity is the entrance to transforming one's own thinking—and, as a result, transforming one's community. Education has a primary role in this. Educators, parents, administrators, as well as others outside of the schools (chapter 1), can create the conditions for creativity to emerge from individual learners. Teaching for creative thinking is possible (chapter 6, "Education for Creative Problem Solving").

Bleedorn's career and continued work in this field proves this. The stories in this book are stories of hope that imagination can be developed, shared, and directed for improving our individual and collective quality of life.

Bleedorn demonstrates throughout these pages that creativity matters. It matters for the economy (chapter 7, "Creativity = Capital"), which grows and develops as a result of ideas—and suffers for lack of ideas. It matters for democracies (chapter 12, "Education for Democracy"), both for forming new ones and maintaining existing ones. It matters for communities (chapter 9, "The Evolution of a Global Intellect"), which become more resourceful and resilient when creative thinking is tapped. It matters for the environment (chapter 10, "How Green Was My Planet"), which thrives when we can visualize the interconnectedness of our planet.

Skills for improving the quality of thinking are needed throughout the world. Bleedorn reminds us of this early in her preface with the words of Buckminster Fuller: "If humanity is to pass safely through the present crisis on earth, it will be because a majority of individuals are now doing their own thinking."

Bleedorn sits us down on the magic carpet of imagination and takes us through the profound journey that creative education can have in preparing students (chapter 4, "Habits of Thought") to possess and live their own creative mind-set, thus becoming productive workers and contributing citizens. In his essay "On Creativity," the physicist David Bohm describes this "creative state of mind" that is necessary for creative work.

> The creative state of mind is . . . one whose interest in what is being done is wholehearted and total, like that of a young child. With this spirit, it is always open to learning what is new, to perceiving new differences and new similarities, leading to new orders and structures, rather than always tending to impose familiar orders and structures in the field of what is seen. (Bohm 1998)

Bleedorn applies her creative state of mind to the state of education in our society and to the impact that creatively educated citizens can have in transforming their communities. Throughout this book, she considers education, business, politics, society, economics, history, science, and the environment and weaves the golden thread of creativity across these diverse fields—arguing that education programs can be "designed to make the best possible use of the natural power of the human mind to grow and develop and to be significantly active in service to a cause beyond oneself. . . . There are no limits to the intellectual resource of the human mind when it is provided with an atmosphere and support for personal growth."

All of us have a stake in applying our own creative strengths to the task of engaging the creativity of our world's children throughout their lifelong educational experiences. This task frequently puts us at odds with the "norms" of society. Creativity, for some, is a subversive concept. Those who advocate for more creativity may feel like an outsider in their cause. In these pages, we are urged, if necessary, to be willing to be "a minority of one" in order to promote creative thinking.

This feeling is not foreign to Bleedorn. She knows firsthand what Dorothee Sölle describes as "creative disobedience." In her book by that title, Sölle writes, "Beyond obedience there is resistance. . . . Imagination is needed and new forms of disobedience are required for the struggles to come."

Bleedorn has been a pioneering futurist when it comes to anticipating and articulating the struggles in education. She's known intuitively in her own experience and explicitly in the classrooms and workplaces in which she's found herself, that creatively engaged students, teachers, and communities can transcend the challenges and limitations they experience every day (appendix C, "Statements of Students").

Bleedorn is not afraid in these writings to resist the education system that we know today. She's not afraid to inspire everyone's imagination—inside and outside of the school—to be applied when it comes to educating for enlightened and engaged citizenship.

Bleedorn's "disobedience" in the educational reform debate that is prominent in this book is not new in her life. Yet most of the rest of us are still challenged to discover ways that our "creative disobedience" can impact learners so that, ultimately, we all contribute to the well-being of our global society. *Education Is Everybody's Business: A Wake-Up Call to Advocates of Educational Change* gives us the courage and the motivation to "disobey."

Bleedorn's style is to draw out the strengths and passions of those she interacts with, whether it's a student in the classroom, a musician at a jazz bar, a person standing next to her in line, or the reader of her ideas. This book takes that same approach, encouraging people across disciplines to unlock their creativity, to build on what works, to seek new partnerships, and to transcend their differences.

One of the basic tenets of brainstorming and creative problem solving is to piggyback or build on others' ideas. Bleedorn does not seek to discount the education work currently being done but to build upon the best of what is occurring, while simultaneously suggesting different structures from which new educational models could emerge.

The proposition Bleedorn presents here builds on the work of many brilliant thinkers—ranging from Thomas Jefferson to creativity pioneers Paul Torrance, Alex Osborn, Ruth Noller, and Sidney Parnes to economist Richard Florida to educational psychologists Howard Gardner and Robert Sternberg to German artist Joseph Beuys. In turn, we are challenged to build on Bleedorn's, our colleagues', and our own ideas to deepen the impact of creativity across the education system and ultimately in society at large.

Bleedorn has dedicated her career to helping people uncover what is already inside them—the power to use their creativity to improve the quality of their thinking for the betterment of their lives, their organizations, and society in general. *Education Is Everybody's Business: A Wake-Up Call to Advocates of Educational Change* is a comprehensive guide to unlocking the creative mind and to reaching across the planet to make it better for "all its passengers."

Many often perceive this as lofty or idealistic, much like many may perceive Bleedorn's appeal in this book—that everybody should make the creative education of youth their business—but her ideas are very real-world. They will ignite your imagination and inspire you to connect in real ways with the education system yourself, whether it is by helping your own children unleash their creative strengths; by becoming a mentor to other children; by running for your local school board; by linking the worlds of business, education, and government in your community; by advocating for creative education in newspaper editorials; or by sharing the power of your own creativity with others.

By making education *her* business, Bleedorn has touched the lives of many and they have been forever changed by her and her message. Now, you are invited to be touched and changed by Bleedorn's powerful ideas—and in the process, make education *your* business.

Steven Dahlberg
General manager, Creative Education Foundation
January 2005

PREFACE: EDUCATION IS EVERYBODY'S BUSINESS

If humanity is to pass safely through the present crisis on earth, it will be because a majority of individuals are now doing their own thinking.

—Buckminster Fuller

Some years ago, R. Buckminster Fuller (1977) gave us the message. He told us that society was becoming so specialized that we were in danger of losing our capacity as a people to integrate the specializations into a shared system. He was right, not only about society in general but also about the institution of education upon which so much of society's values depend.

Education has been the centerpiece of my entire professional life. My experiences have included service across an entire spectrum of educational perspectives—from teaching in a one-room rural school to a state educational consultantship, university professorship, and public speaker for business and other organizations. As an "educational entrepreneur," I designed and initiated programs and college courses in creativity studies and futures studies. In the process, I have been privileged to exchange ideas, not only with academicians and professionals of many stripes but also with a cross section of informed and concerned citizens.

In recent years, it has become quite clear that the institution of education was creating a great deal of discontent both within the halls of ivy and outside of the centers of power throughout society. Calls for educational reform have reached a new level of attention politically, and government has been treating the problem as if more money and smaller classes would solve everything. The mentality that the only realities are the ones that are countable and measurable is inadequate when the problems are more humanistically qualitative than scientifically quantitative. Issues of bureaucratic administration practices, standardization of student assessment, high school dropout rates, unrealized potential, cultural diversity, achievement tests, and questions about what is taught and how it is taught—all have come under the scrutiny of a concerned public.

It is becoming increasingly evident that traditional practices of standardized teaching and assessment no longer serve the learning needs of an intellectually, economically, culturally, physically, and emotionally divergent population of learners. Gary Jedynak (2005), in an unpublished paper on "Science, Education, and Self Assessment," reports a most encouraging educational trend. The development of self-assessment inventories is making its way into educational practices. Based on work by Grant Wiggins (1998), the report by Jedynak holds promise of doing a better job of "mapping the territory of human potential." If students could learn to "map" their own knowledge and take greater control over their future, we could, in time, expect the end of standardized, quantitative, competitive grading.

It is fair to acknowledge that radical changes in society have added to the usual challenges of educators. Economic pressures, greater cultural diversity in school populations, less respect for authority, and computerized learning and its trend toward depersonalization of schooling are examples of the growing complexities of teaching and learning. Something needs to be done to restore a more positive relationship between school and society. The general opinion seems to be that major change cannot occur voluntarily from action within the system. Harlan Cleveland, an authority on leadership, said, as far back as 1984, that "most of the real leadership in promoting new policies comes from activist citizens, men and women who are not preoccupied with formal power or getting their names in the newspaper—people whose concern exceeds even their confusion" (Cleveland 1984, 2).

Certainly there is plenty of confusion to go around. There is also energy and a commitment to education—and that is the reason for this book. My listening post and my observations from the arena of public affairs are telling me that change agents within educational institutions and citizens with an awareness of the complexities inherent in educational leadership can combine their efforts and make a difference.

As a semiretired educationist, I have tried to produce a book that reminds us of the noble purposes of public education expressed by Thomas Jefferson (1899) at the beginning of our history. Thomas Jefferson left no doubt that a functioning democracy depended upon an educated electorate. The world has changed radically since his time, but that basic fact remains. Unless the public mind and voice can function with an independent quality that transcends the motivation for narrow, self-serving interests, a true democracy cannot survive. The limited number of citizens who go to the polls and take advantage of their voting privilege testifies to a limited educational preparation for an active role in a democracy. Being an informed and independent thinker is another hoped-for mentality in a voter. Casting a vote based on some emotional personal response to an ideological matter without the understanding of the entire governmental system of balance between rights and responsibilities weakens a democracy as well as a world order.

Because my academic background in educational psychology, leadership, and human behavior includes a focus on the discipline of creative education, the chapters in this book reflect that connection. The understanding of the value of creative thinking in education and society has caused me to argue also for the importance of other higher order thinking processes in the school experience.

The arrival of the Information Age has created an explosion of available facts and figures. The capacity to process the Information Age overload requires independent, complex thinking at levels of global systems, transformations, and vision. The fact that these thinking processes can be specifically taught has critical importance to educational service for a dynamically changing society and world order. There is an additional value in the by-product of complex thinking exercises in school curricula at all levels of learning—the discovery and identification of students already practiced in the art of higher-order thinking. Recognizing and capitalizing on that level of intellect would be a service to students as well as to society.

Parents of smart kids understand the need such students have to get beyond the accumulation of facts to schooling that challenges the mind and stimulates the spirit. Many high school dropout problems could be better understood and avoided if opportunities to think and be heard were provided regularly in every classroom where creative teaching was a regular practice.

The common thread in these chapters is the hope that educational programs will become better designed to make the best possible use of the natural power of the human mind to grow and develop and to be significantly active in service to a cause beyond oneself. Although some of Earth's resources are limited, there are no limits to the intellectual resource of the human mind when it is provided with an atmosphere and support for personal growth.

The major purpose of this book, then, is to attract readership among enlightened educators and the general public alike so that the relationship between education and society will be fortified, and new integrated leadership for enlightened education will emerge.

It may be that the singular quality of my educational journey has been a unique preparation for perceiving possibilities for new ways of dealing with the challenges of education for a fully functioning democracy. I have never felt like an ordinary educator. Setting out in middle age to acquire a series of degrees while serving educational institutions was somewhat unusual at the time that I began the long-delayed pursuit of a college degree. Let me explain with a bit of personal history.

When I graduated from high school with a good academic record and an appetite for advanced learning and a career in journalism, our single-parent family resources were limited to a degree that the only alternative was a year of preparation for rural school teaching. A few years later, I added a year at a teacher's college. That two-year teaching certificate followed me through years of marriage, which put me in the constant company of school officials and their wives, all of whom had college degrees. I knew from the beginning that my intellectual capacities were worthy of official recognition, and when the chance came, I responded to the leadership of E. Paul Torrance in creative education and put my energies into joining his work to help create education with a built-in understanding of creative and intellectual potential in all students.

In addition, I have, for better or worse, been cursed (or blessed) with such a strong inclination for connection-making that I have dipped into a cross section of educational and social developments reflected in articles on global education, environmental sustainability, futures studies, leadership, technological society, problem solving, and educational change. The book has become a staging area for the focus of attention that is central to the chapters in this book. That focus is the critical need for new ways of thinking in and about the world and the combined action of school and society that will get us there.

A poem written for me by a student at Metropolitan State University in the early 1970s gives the reason for this project:

> Seed Woman
> Sower of potential humans,
> Like a chemist
> You experiment with possibilities
> And mix together the unordinary
> Until it becomes the extraordinary.
>
> We will always need in this world
> Flowers and roots, seeds and ground,
> and a sower—whether it be the wind
> Or you.

ACKNOWLEDGMENTS

This book is the natural result of years of serious thinking about education and wondering why it is that—in spite of the scores of dedicated teachers, vigorous research projects and advanced-degree theses, years of concentrated study, huge sums of money, a trend toward ultramodern, efficient facilities, a highly organized system of operation, and a concerned public—something in the educational establishment is not working according to plan. Too many students are being poorly served, too many good teachers become discouraged and leave, new ideas for reform are traditionally lost in bureaucratic tangles, and the percentage of voters exercising their privilege of living in a democracy is painfully low.

Personal observations from within the system and years of conversations with a cross section of concerned citizens have persuaded me that a potential force for meaningful change is available. When the possibilities for improved education at all levels can be recognized in the public sector and integrated with that of enlightened educators within the system, positive change *is* possible. When the will to act is added, it is even probable.

The reader will recognize the fact that this collection of articles has the mark of a personal journey. There has been little specific help or interference from outside sources to report. Because of a wealth of information and philosophies accumulated over forty years of professional activity, the ideas here have been emerging independently for a long time. They have been influenced and strengthened recently by the increased dissatisfaction with education expressed by professionals and public alike in news articles, journals, organizations, and public platforms. Therefore, an acknowledgment is due the entire collection of thought leaders in school and society who have been contributing to the *zeitgeist* for educational reform.

One very specific acknowledgment goes to Dr. Patience Dirkx for her most valuable support and service in the preparation of the manuscript for publication. Her special skills have translated my writing into a carefully formatted document ready for the publisher. In addition, her professional judgment has been consistently available when uncertainties regarding details needed an objective opinion. In spite of a heavy demand on her time, she made herself available for discussions and even finished the work before deadline. Our years of friendship and her continuous encouragement for my ideas regarding education are appreciated beyond measure.

There will always be reasons for remembering and acknowledging past understanding and support for my entrepreneurial activities in education from officials like Monsignor Terrence Murphy during the years of his presidency at the University of St. Thomas in St. Paul, Minnesota, and from Dr. William Salesses, former dean of the Graduate School of Education at that institution. Also Derald Erdman, former director of the Entrepreneurship Program at St. Thomas, opened the doors of opportunity to design and teach courses in creative problem solving as a required course in the entrepreneurship program. Earl Belisle of the St. Thomas Research Library staff added his expert service whenever I needed help with obscure information and research findings. Seventeen years at the University of St. Thomas strengthened my belief in the value of creative studies and futures studies in both education and business departments in higher education, and fortified my resolve to continue my work through the avenue of writing.

A long list of friends and colleagues deserves mention for their support and for their own contributions to the promotion of educational change of the creative kind: Piet Muller, Angel Sanhueza, Efiong Etuk,

Steve Dahlberg, Frank Maraviglia, Garnet Millar, Ray Anderson, Barbara Gilles, Marilyn Fiedler, Christina Coyle, Louise Loomis, Dorie Shallcross, Gary Jedynak, Gus Jaccaci, Marie Manthey, Charles Remke, Robert Brown, and many more.

Finally, my everlasting thanks to my daughters, Joan Barnes and Bonnie Sample, who have endorsed all of my educational initiatives and who can always be depended upon for the best kind of encouragement and good cheer.

❶

INTRODUCTION

There is an urgent need for educational programs that lead to discovery and do not stop at instruction; that encourage insights, not merely the accumulation of information, and that foster personal involvement rather than passive emulation.

—Ervin Laszlo

Our society has made no secret of the fact that getting a good education has a lot to do with the quality of one's life. Very few would dispute that claim. But not very many would think beyond the credo and begin to wonder what really constitutes a good education. A standard perception of "education" for most people probably fits a dictionary definition that declares education to be "instruction or training by which people develop and learn to use their mental, moral, and physical powers."

There was a time when the judgment of educational policymakers was trusted to decide what would be taught and how the training and instruction would be delivered. But something happened when the developments of science and technology created a different kind of world. Instead of a life of neighborhood dimensions and countries within borders, we all became part of a dynamically changing, intercultural global family, living in a complex international system. We changed almost everything *except* the way we think.

Now the new kind of world is making new demands on those mental powers. Every fully functioning person—young, old, and in between—is affected in some ways by his or her membership in a radically changing society and its uncertain future. The scope of our awareness has been expanded to include the state of affairs anywhere on the planet. For anyone engaged in creating a personal and family life, the challenges of a changing, shifting landscape generate constant demands on the mental powers for making choices, planning ahead, solving problems, and dealing effectively with new learning, new experiences, and new ways of thinking.

When educational programs for cultivating mental, moral, and physical powers are analyzed, the exercise of physical powers scores high in today's society. Physical education, sports, and games at every level of learning are an essential part of the school experience. In some cases, sports programs play a dominant role in the program at the expense of other more enduring personal developments. American society has continued the emphasis on physical conditioning to a degree that could create a serious imbalance between values placed on body-building and values related to mind-building.

The moral component of education's delivery system has to be strongly related to the mental component. How we use our mental power makes a big difference in the actions we take. The mind processes the available information and arrives at a decision. Behavior can be said to depend upon the quality of our thinking. Vincent Ruggiero (1988) has reminded us that "thinking is an art with its own purposes, standards, principles, rules, strategies, and precautions. And it is an art well worth learning, for every important thing we do is affected by our habits of mind" (1). Limitations in the quality of thinking can produce judgments and behaviors that fail to understand the affected scope and the possible future effects of our actions. If instruction and training in the use of mental, moral, and physical powers defines education, it would be fair to suggest that news stories are providing ample evidence that the mental and moral powers of many graduates of educational institutions have failed the moral part of training and instruction. The appearance of *The Cheating Culture* (Callahan 2004) casts a shadow over the highly successful careers of some university graduates.

In spite of all the astonishing developments of science and technology, computerized global communication, space discoveries, research and development across disciplines, and the breaking of records of physical prowess, reports of development on the mental and moral side of the human equation are in short supply. The news media reports evidence of corruption in business, problems of truth in advertising, cheating in schools, violence in society, excessive materialism, hypocrisy in politics, and more. Add to these the fact of a low turnout of voters in the election process, and it would seem to recall the words of Thomas Jefferson, "I know no safe depository of the ultimate powers of the society but the people themselves; and if we think them not enlightened enough to exercise their control with a wholesome discretion, the remedy is not to take it from them, but to inform their discretion by education" (1889, 161).

If Thomas Jefferson is right and the people themselves have the ultimate power in a democratic society, their mental development has to keep pace with the complexities of the changing scene. A diploma or certificate in any special field is no guarantee of a lifetime of reasoned judgment in an interrelated, interactive system. Buckminster Fuller (1977) once observed that the trend toward intense specialization in education and society was failing to provide for the consideration of systemic realities. One criticism of education being made by the people is the failure to teach the integration of special fields of study with the broader collection of knowledge. There is an urgent need for mentalities that can *see the big picture* and have some time reality in the future.

The traditional organizational structure of academia—with its focus on specializations and specific requirements—can produce competition between separate departments for students, for money, for status, for publicity, and for honors in the field. Efforts at integrative education suffer from the fixation of many educators on one specific discipline. Integrative education is needed to prepare the public mind for the art of realistic, systemic thinking. Isolation tactics in the real world are counterproductive. The lesson shouldn't have to be learned through experience or intuition. Integrative learning and thinking can take place in the process of formal, mandated education.

An opportunity exists for concerned citizens to influence educational programs in new directions. Public opinion and recommendations based on real-world experiences can have real value for educational policymakers. Education, and especially higher education, needs more input from practitioners of every discipline in the outside world. Open minds and open systems are, of course, a necessary prerequisite. With serious initiative and a little bit of luck, schools can become a place where students' assessment of learning is based not only on their memory but also on how well they have learned to think.

Another source of valuable advice is in the great number of dedicated and informed teachers and administrators within the system whose ideas for educational improvement often have difficulty being heard in a hierarchical system of management. The popular inclination to assess learning through standardized tests places a burden on teachers who are often forced to teach to the test, administer the test, score the test, and report the test instead of using the time to provide learning activities that engage the minds and attention of students. Officials dedicated to numbering and counting deflect the school experience away from the human component and the reality of diverse talents and learning styles. Who is shortchanged in an autocratic, standardized, immovable system? The customers—a.k.a. the students.

There can be little argument with the claim that the urge to learn, to grow, and to be recognized is a natural, inherent quality in almost everyone at any age. That urge can be lost when the school routine provides no opportunity for self-expression along with the discipline of prescriptive learning. Discipline and competitive accountability by numbers without some avenue for satisfaction and personal significance in the daily program can account for many kinds of problems. Feelings and attitudes, uncountable as they are, have an equal place in the formula for school success. Parents watching a son or daughter fail or become disenchanted with the life at school can be strongly motivated to work for changes in schooling. The voices of parents, PTA members, school boards, and other community groups are beginning to be heard and to find ways to express their concern to the powers that be. They need to be encouraged to find ways to unite and to make their recommendations for educational updating known and considered.

There may be reasons for the dependence of some educators on quantitative assessment figures. It may be that teacher and administrative education courses pay too little attention to studies of human behavior and human diversity. In spite of research findings that define differences in learning and thinking styles, an official priority of teaching to the standardized test can become an extremely poor translation of educational excellence. It may be that educators are so programmed by the focus on research in their preparation for teaching that they hesitate to make a personal judgment without the security of proof in the numbers and statistical matrix to support their observations.

A certain amount of testing is considered a normal part of schooling. Diagnostic testing can be especially essential for teaching and learning effectiveness. But government-mandated requirements like the No Child Left Behind federal program for excessive counting, measuring, and categorizing of students for statistical purposes is burdensome to the spirit of learning. Strict bureaucratic procedures for competitive public record keeping have been described as a punitive assault on public education, designed to throw the system into turmoil.

Citizens who raise a public voice about such abuses of authority serve a democratic system well. There is little reason for them to be intimidated and silenced by authoritarian educational demands. The original purpose of education to provide a place of growth and development for a diverse population of future voters can be distorted by too much number crunching and labeling of students.

Official policymakers can profit by changing from traditional top-down management to a more inclusive form of leadership (more later on leadership). Concerned citizens have a right to think and be heard, especially when issues of education impact so directly on their lives, the lives of their children, and the strength of a democracy. The voice of the people becomes more important as information becomes more available to everyone and the arena of human affairs aspires to continue its evolution to higher mental and moral ground.

Traditional education under the control of officially certified professionals falls easily into education designed by old habits of thought and procedures. Faculty with the security of tenure are often seen to favor the traditional standards and practices of educating that require no challenges of change or risk taking on the part of the educator. But enlightened and informed educators with a commitment to student development and individual potential in a changing world need a measure of freedom to appeal to the powers that be for adjustments in the system. The practice of rewarding the compliant and ignoring or punishing the independent thinker perpetuates a static system.

A closed system of organization in institutionalized education with no upward communication possibilities is a serious frustration to teachers of excellence, and can result in the loss of valuable educational capital. Good teachers can become so discouraged by constraints on their natural teaching style that they walk away from their chosen profession. The damage can be just as real when good teachers, for economic reasons, try to absorb the frustration and continue to teach. The mismatch between officially mandated requirements for the classroom and a teacher's personal urge for a more flexible, student-oriented, effective learning environment results in a constant state of tension for many educators. The unavoidable loss of spirit and sense of support can be as real as any measurable factor in the quality of performance in the classroom.

When tenured faculty in higher education settle into the comfort zone of "business as usual," the loss to educational vitality can be just as costly as absolute job security anywhere in the workplace. In addition to the benefits of college and university tenure, there is often the additional advantage of service on committees significant to a particular academic discipline and/or to university operations and policies. As in K–12 education, there are likely to be many student-oriented professors with ideas for new courses, new ways of integrating learning, of exercising flexibility in requirements, of responding to new developments in the realm of human affairs beyond the ivy-covered institution. Even when a structure exists for influencing the program, the unspoken academic politics and the competition between educators and departments can create a defense against new ideas.

Of course, the present system has served many students well. The professions have benefited from many examples of outstanding scholarship throughout the entire collection of specializations. Many graduates across the spectrum of disciplines have performed well, accomplished much in the world of work, and created envious levels of fame and fortune in their field. However, the expectation that a good education would result in an enviable quality of life has been a disappointment in many cases. Somehow, the focus on competition and individual success has trumped our necessary attention to the human commons. Studies of human behavior and potential, human diversity and development, philosophy, the integration of specializations, the ethics of business, peace and justice, or environmental sustainability—the values that are enduring to the human condition—have had to take second place to departments of science and technology, business management, statistics, and whatever else is seen as guaranteeing opportunities for big money and enviable social status.

Public opinion is realizing like never before that the quality of life depends not only on personal income, social position, and material wealth but also on the general quality of the entire arena of human affairs in the world. There is increasing public opinion that the current educational system is in serious need of reform if Thomas Jefferson (1899) was right when he spoke of the importance of an educated electorate. His definition of education could not have predicted the kind of world that has developed since his time. His perceptions of what would be taught, how it would be taught, and who would teach it would have to undergo a makeover. However, his observations on education continue to be realistic about the need for an educated public in service to a democracy. He certainly got that right.

Developments in alternative education send a clear message to public education. Homeschooling, transfers to private schools, increasing numbers of charter schools, distance learning, and more are practicing organizational and teaching strategies that provide for greater diversity of student interests and more opportunities for independent and team experiential learning. Students whose educational needs are not being met and who are disenchanted with traditional schooling in many public education settings find alternative education programs a better fit for their aspirations. Dedicated educators with ideas for creative teaching in a system that offers more flexibility and personal choice appreciate the more open-ended structure of charter schools. The expectation is that public education will adopt some of the motivational strategies of teaching and learning practiced in charter school programs. Flexibility and standards of performance are not mutually exclusive.

Direct involvement of students in learning and thinking activities are central to many alternative schools. A very basic learning theory known as the Cone of Experience and introduced some years ago by Fantini and Weinstein (1969) has had some circulation but little application in authoritarian school settings. Their work features the concept of providing a direct, purposeful experience for students as an introduction to new learning units. After participation in meaningful experiential learning activities related to the material to be studied, the learning is more readily absorbed and remembered.

The seminal work of Dr. E. Paul Torrance on creative education and his *Incubation Model of Teaching* (Torrance and Safter 1990) has for many years been providing understanding and guidelines for teaching that engages the student mind in creative thinking and motivates learning in diverse populations (more later about the contributions of Paul Torrance).

Philosophers like Teilhard de Chardin (1961) have reminded us that the human intellect is by its nature forever in the process of evolving to higher levels of complexity. Alert minds engage readily in the process. Attention to new knowledge and the nature of the world around them creates new connections, new insights, and new ideas from outside of the structure. There has been enough despair on the part of educational change agents to affect the bureaucracy of the educational establishment—but the degree of uncertainty in the state of the world stacked against the hope of its future as a friendly, healthy place is new to our awareness.

There is a growing sensation that something very important is trying to happen in the world. It can't happen without a more effective role of education in providing instruction and training in the development of mental, moral, and physical powers. The concerned public will need to step up its efforts to break through the defenses inherent in the historically structured system of public education. Educational entrepreneurs are desperately needed both inside and outside the establishment.

The business world places a serious value on the quality of creativity and innovation as a factor in vitalizing the work place and increasing revenue. On the other hand, there is a tendency in business circles to dismiss the academic world as "too theoretical" and "too impractical." The popular position has been to perceive a polarization between academia and the "real world."

The business community is in a strategic position to team up with educational policymakers for serious academic programs that provide the understanding and cultivation of creative and other complex thinking systems as basic requirements for effective functioning in the world of work. Corporations would save money if they didn't have to budget for independent consultants to provide for the discovery and stimulation of creative thinking in the workforce (more later on creativity and capital).

The press also has the potential to contribute to a better understanding of the need for new ways of thinking in educational programs and in the marketplace. Particularly, the simplistic perception of the popular term "creativity" as related only to artistic expression needs to be expanded. Then the proper perception of creativity in the public mind will come to include the full force of its more sophisticated, theoretical application across the full spectrum of human intellectual capacities.

There is growing evidence that the public is increasingly aware of its stake in the quality of education at every level of learning. One way to make a difference is to campaign and lobby education policymakers and political power bases for

- Opening the closed system for more communication up, down, and sideways between policymakers and concerned public.
- Creating more balance between quantitative measurement of learning and the uncountable qualitative factors of human intellectual and psychological development.
- Connecting the lofty learning of traditional academe to the reality of a world in transition economically, environmentally, socially, and in every other way.
- Increasing academic authority for the deliberate teaching of quality, higher-order thinking at all levels of education.

Remember that education doesn't have all the answers. The world needs a good measure of answers that extend beyond research results to the uncountable qualities of wisdom, fairness, vision, and an active conscience.

2

EDUCATION: UNDERSTAND IT
BACKWARDS, LIVE IT FORWARDS

Innovation requires a trust in the future that is difficult to arouse or sustain in organizations constantly looking to the past. Living with change need not imply insecurity, but rather developing new forms of security.

—Rosabeth Moss Kanter

A friend gave me a poster with a quotation from the work of Kierkegaard: "Life must be understood backwards, but it must be lived forwards." The same wisdom can be applied to the institution of education. The historical record of the development of modern educational systems has relevance to the vision of future learning that will serve not only individual development but will also specifically serve a transforming society in its quest for a better, more peaceful world.

Education has to be more than learning the skills and knowledge that can be passed on from the mind of one person into the mind of another. Scholars from times as early as those of St. Thomas Aquinas understood that the teacher must not be pictured as pouring his knowledge into the learner "as though particles of the same knowledge could pass from one subject to another." At its best, education includes the specific understanding and exercise of the art of thinking (more about that later).

Understanding education backwards would have to begin with the storytellers of early primitive people. In the tribal life of early civilizations, learning was by example and instruction in skills for survival. Leaders emerged and became authorities. Individual talents developed and were recognized for their service to the tribe and their adherence to tribal values. Much later, when written language appeared, the scholars and scribes represented the centers of learning. The monks of the early church were regarded as fountains of wisdom.

When the invention of the printing press made reading available to more people, learning took on a new dimension. Knowledge was no longer reserved for the privileged elite. Learning systems dependent upon an authority were now augmented by the option of independent learning. The choice of learning a trade under the guidance of a guild master or mentor now had an alternative. Students and scholars with access to books had open doors to unlimited learning and independent thinking in pursuit of personal interests and aptitudes. The distinction between the literate and illiterate members of society created a framework for social class identity.

Then came the Industrial Revolution. Piet Muller (2003) made a relevant observation on its significance to education:

> Public education as we know it today is a product of the Industrial Revolution. In spite of the fact that the world has changed dramatically, the aim and the ethos of the education system are in many ways exactly the same as 300 years ago: to send children to school for twelve years in order to produce people capable of working for someone else without asking too many questions. (ix)

Of course, the foregoing observations on education have their base primarily in Western civilization. The developments of learning and thinking in other parts of the world would have their own stories. Countries that identify with the cultures of the East and Middle East would follow different paths and timelines. Education in African nations would reflect the design of education according to that of the territorial governments. People in Spanish-speaking lands would have an educational history with Latin influences. Areas in the world like the outback of Australia or the frozen Arctic or remote Pacific Islands would have other descriptions of their educational and social development.

The common thread would probably be evidence of a common human urge in most people to grow, to learn, to investigate, to express themselves, to achieve and be recognized, and to contribute in some way to the community. Being recognized for that contribution is part of the reward system and part of the motivation to invest oneself in the learning process.

In the original centers of learning, an additional factor was present. Early teaching through the guidance and example of masters created a meaningful human presence for the learner that provided standards of excellence in their learning expectations and achievements. In the guilds of the Middle Ages, learning engaged students in real, hands-on projects that combined the reality of the senses and the organic world with the imaginative vision of the final product. Much of learning was individualized and personalized. The arts and crafts of the old world testify to the excellence of student work.

One of the best examples of early public education in American history was the one-room school of pioneer times. That model continued to serve rural communities in many parts of the country until at least the middle of the twentieth century. The following description of the American one-room rural school is drawn from my personal experience as a country schoolteacher in Minnesota from 1930–1933. Not many in our current society would have any understanding of the significant levels of learning that took place in a country school. Not many could easily believe that the limited facilities could support the level of physical, intellectual, and moral development that students demonstrated.

My home was in a small town two miles from the gray stucco schoolhouse that was something of a family icon, since my great-aunt Margaret, my mother, and my older sister had all taught there earlier. My grandmother also had been a pupil there (District 46, Carver County, Minnesota) in pioneer times. Because we were a no-car family, I walked to and from school when I wasn't lucky enough to catch a ride along the way. In the winter I built the fire in the pot-bellied stove in the center of the schoolroom when I arrived. In extreme winter weather, I paid a lad from a neighboring farm to get a fire started before I came.

There were days in the middle of winter when the ink in the ink wells of the student desks was frozen in the morning and didn't thaw out until noon.

There were about twenty students from grades 2 to 8 every year in the school. Plumbing was outside. Water was drawn from a pump on the grounds and carried in a pail to the cloak hall. Children drank from a common dipper. Lunch was carried from home in a pail or lunch box. There were large portraits of Washington and Lincoln on the wall, and a wall clock, a globe, a set of maps, and blackboards across the front of the room provided the basic instructional needs. A hand-held bronze bell with a clear and unmistakable message called the students in from the playground at nine o'clock. At four o'clock, the school day ended (except for the times that threatening weather changed the schedule). A short recess was usually scheduled midmorning and midafternoon. Time out for lunch and recreation usually happened from about twelve to one. So much for the statistics.

What happened within that basic structure of time and material was a wealth of learning. In addition to the educational outcomes of students, teaching in a country school provided some educational observations that could still be guidelines for learning anywhere. Here are a few.

- Effective learning happens even when children are not categorized by age and deliberately taught and tested on material officially appropriate for their age level. Unintended learning by osmosis when listening and observing whatever is going on around them is not programmed for in tests and measurements of achievement. It doesn't appear in records, but it is just as real as the official scorecard and often better remembered. The factors of personal interest, choice, and the absence of pressure and competition to perform create the best learning situation for some individual learning styles.
- Special projects and programs that discover individual talents and provide for creative expression of ideas spark the spirit and create mutual respect in the learning community.
- Occasional visits from outside of the community (in this case, the county superintendent of schools) were motivators for both teacher and students to be recognized for good work.
- The school district was governed by elected members of the district. They were available, along with parents and other members of the community, for services like setting up a "stage" for the

Christmas program and organizing the district picnic in the spring. The total public support and appreciation for the affairs of the school and the achievement of the students was never in doubt. The integration of home, school, and community was a powerful feature of rural school effectiveness and, I might add, for the comfort and satisfaction of the teacher.

- It was my good fortune to have a number of children in that school who sang well, so music was a part of the school day with accompaniment on an old (now antique) organ. Pumping the organ by means of foot pedals took a lot of energy, but it did the job.

- The day was organized around ten-minute classes by grades. There were daily assignments and papers to correct. Report cards were issued every month. Older students and siblings were eager to help the younger ones with reading and arithmetic drills. Learning was integrative, interdisciplinary, and intergenerational.

- Holidays were observed with special programs. Physical education was outside in the schoolyard playing games, often supervised by older students. Students were generally happy and healthy. I don't remember any serious behavior problems. In the winter and during harvest season, attendance of some of the older students was often irregular enough to seriously interrupt their learning. In the spring, students competed in a "Play Day" with other country schools in the county. Some students competed in the annual county declamation contest. Outstanding student artwork and other projects were selected for display and competition at the Minnesota State Fair.

- For the teacher, the day was an exercise in total authority and responsibility to deal with emergencies of injuries and illness or threatening weather. There was no telephone or nearby farmhouse. My salary was around $100 a month. The system worked well. I believe we thought of ourselves as a team. We earned the approval of parents and community and trusted each other to "bring honor to the tribe."

In 1934, the requirement for teaching in a town school was a two-year teaching certificate offered by teacher colleges. My certificate from St. Cloud Teachers College in Minnesota qualified me to teach in a typical small town of the period, Belle Plaine, Minnesota. In addition to serious attention to academic outcomes, the principles of teaching in the seventh- and eighth-grade classroom had much in common with teaching anywhere: respect for student diversities, the establishment of a climate of cooperation as opposed to competition, the expectation of positive academic and social performance, mutual trust, and a policy of not "sweating the small stuff."

The big difference was being in a situation with a qualified administrator who spared the teacher from the anxiety of isolation and total responsibility. Like Belle Plaine, most small towns were happy to include teachers in the social life of the churches and other local organizations. Other connections to the community came with the arrangement to rent a room with a local family. There was a certain amount of public attention to the personal life of the local teacher, including the assumption that teachers were not to be seen smoking or drinking in public. They were expected to set proper behavior examples for local students.

State board examinations checked on the quality of teaching and learning. Sport teams and local events excited community spirit and provided for intergenerational socializing. A beginning salary was $100 a month with a $5.00 raise after the first year if the teaching performance met the approval of the school board. Teachers enjoyed the respect of the community and the students. There were no major behavior problems except for an occasional report of student drinking or smoking in the high school. The use of drugs had not arrived on the scene. Looking back, it seemed like a time of innocence except for occasional pranks— like the time a few high school boys sneaked up on our Girl Scout moonlight campfire along the river, appearing suddenly out of the dark and causing a panic.

The period of the 1960s brought social changes that had a lasting impact on public education. The disruptive effect of public protests against the Vietnam War, the development of an antiestablishment culture, and women's liberation were among social changes that left their mark on college campuses and, in turn, on education in general. With women working outside of the home, the traditional security of a consistent adult presence was often lost, along with much of the traditional parental guidance and support. The addition of new and diverse cultures to school populations and the growing number of economically deprived students created additional challenges. It began to seem that society was having more impact on education than education was having on society.

Then there was the arrival on the educational scene of new technology that ushered in a new age of learning. Fascination with computer-assisted learning, information retrieval, and the opportunities for independent and distance learning had a stunning effect on the process of educating. The magic of the machine had more appeal than the magic and potential of the human mind. The rush to the modern world often has little respect for past arts and beliefs, and substitutes the "technology and god of materialism" for the rich diversity of cultures. The jury is still out for a verdict on the question: "Does technology reduce our capacity to think?"

If the cultivation of mental, moral, and physical powers remains the purpose of public education, achievement of the purpose remains speculative. The need for public concern about achievement of those purposes is greater that ever before. The vision and judgment of concerned citizens regarding educational policies and regulations have genuine value to officials with power and authority to design learning processes for citizens of a democracy.

Members of society whose perceptions include not only their immediate and personal objectives but also the common good and a vision of the future have a responsibility to participate. They should feel called upon to add their voices to the educational business of thinking forward in time and space and delivering the kind of education that supports the vision of our democratic ideals. Official leadership has an obligation to consider the viewpoints of the electorate when dealing with the sensitive, dynamic social issue of educational reform.

The Education Division of the World Future Society and the International Future Problem-Solving Bowls created by E. Paul Torrance have a history of deliberately teaching the use of the mind that envisions future developments and directions of current trends in society. Quality thinkers of all ages have a natural inclination for a time reality in the future. Effective educational planning requires the exercise of a futuristic brain that can also perceive the broad scope of social change and growth.

Perceiving the natural integration of school and society is a bottom-line requirement for educational reform. The level of uncertainty regarding any prediction of the future is a test of a mentality's tolerance for ambiguity. Visions of educational futures based on current identifiable positive trends can be the start of new, improved directions for all of education. It could be said that planning and predictions require the creative art of "looking into the dark in order to see."

The need for some educational change has become glaringly obvious to anyone concerned with public education. Here are some thoughts on education in the future.

Mortimer Zuckerman, editor-in-chief of *U.S. News and World Report*, provided his insight into educational change in that publication for November 23, 2003. His observation is a long overdue message to legislators and educational officials who control the purse strings. He said, "It's not money or class size that determines how well kids learn. It's cultural attitudes" (84–85). Establishing educational practices based on knowledge of that fact could begin to do away with the inflexibility of numbers and labels that have determined policies for too long. Quantitative measurements that ignore qualitative factors have been the rule for mandated education. It is time to be accountable for the uncountable factors of learning.

Bureaucracies, powerful teachers' unions, and management by a rigid chain of command often deny teachers the freedom to teach and administrators the freedom to administer. A change from traditional authoritarian exclusive management to the inclusive pattern of true leadership would have a profound effect on public schools and their service to students.

The federal mandate of No Child Left Behind has created a firestorm of resistance among serious educators and enlightened public. The idea of basing educational outcomes almost exclusively on standardized tests and basing required learning on the accumulation of facts and memorized history removes from educational purposes the cultivation of the joy of learning, discovery, and of thinking independently. Paul Gruchow, university professor and former chair of the Minnesota Humanities Commission, in an article in the *Minneapolis Star Tribune* (November 25, 2003), offered his vision of schools in which

- Our children learn to think, clearly and with respect for the evidence, for themselves.

- Our children come to know the marvelously rich and varied and colorful cloth from which our culture has been cut.
- Our children come to understand how to turn facts into tools and how to tell the difference between knowledge and wisdom.
- Our children enter the world believing that they can make a difference and that they are equipped with the means to do so.
- Our children catch the sustaining joy of learning. This is, in fact, the greatest gift a teacher has to give. The facts may change, and the details of them will surely fade, but no student ever loses, or fails to profit from, the infectious enthusiasm of a great teacher.

He said further, "This is not a new vision. It is the vision of Thomas Jefferson. It has served us well for more than two centuries. To leave it behind now would be tragically to abandon the very history we propose to teach."

An article in *Atlantic Monthly* (October 2004) made a significant statement about teaching and teachers:

> People working in higher education aren't in it for the money. They care about scholarship; they enjoy working with young people; they believe that what they do matters. That may be why so many of the people we spoke with volunteered that the higher education system was evolving into something less and less connected to any kind of public good. (Fallows and Ganeshananthan 2004, 126)

An operating system that makes use of all the intellectual resources available for student growth and development will, in time, come to replace the inertia of educational bureaucracies. Teacher excellence will flourish because the heart of teaching and the love for students and respect for their diversities will be free to function in classrooms of mutual respect.

Parents and public will realize that education *is* everybody's business. They will be generous with their recommendations to authorities and vigorous in their support for officials who understand what education is all about and will work to make it happen.

3

THE CREATIVITY FACTOR
IN EDUCATION

Creativity is the experience of expressing and actualizing one's individual identity in an integrated form in communion with oneself, with nature, and with other persons.

—Clark Moustakas

I believe that the term *creativity* is one of the most used and least understood words in our culture. My observations also tell me that public interest in creativity in business, in education, and in personal lives is beginning to get the attention it deserves from a variety of perspectives, including a recent announcement of programs on creative aging. In spite of the popularity of its applications, the understanding of the creativity factor as a fundamental human resource worthy of serious study in educational programming has had only limited attention.

The history of the development of the academic discipline of creative studies began fifty years ago and has been promoted somewhat in schools and universities worldwide. However, the popular use of the word *creative* is fairly superficial. Both inside and outside public education little is known or understood about the accumulation of research and resources for creative teaching, identifying and rewarding creative thinking persons in the classroom and throughout society, knowing something about the cognitive (mental) and affective (emotional) factors of the creative process, recognizing the genuinely creative product, or the importance of establishing a climate of trust so critical to creative expression.

While superficial references to creativity as applied to the arts are common in our culture, there is little public knowledge of the substantive nature of the academic discipline of creative studies for which the educational system has responsibility. In some cases, individual teachers or administrators will support or apply teaching strategies that stimulate creative thinking. But a recent search for the mention of creativity in an official set of state educational requirements or standards in social studies found no mention of creative thinking, although a few references to critical, analytical thinking were included in the document.

Most educational centers of power have neglected to acquaint themselves with the academics of creative education, and seem to perceive creativity as related only to the arts and other expendable programs when budgets are tight. That fact underscores the importance of public interest in mandated school curricula. The relative absence of requirements for creative education in official academia suggests that learning and practicing the art of creative thinking is being left largely to chance.

Public attention to the reality of creativity in the public mind took a leap forward with the recent publication of *The Rise of the Creative Class* (2002) by Richard Florida, George Mason University's Hirst Professor of Public Policy. The title sparked immediate public attention. A few years earlier, *The Cultural Creatives: How 50 Million People Are Changing the World* (Ray and Anderson 2000) had awakened the reading public to the fact and value of creative people in changing times. For the first time, the value of creativity was publicly recognized in popular books. However, the major focus of the readings was on the economic value of creative people who are said to be "challenging the structures of 20th century society." It is significant that the value of creativity has been associated with economic profit. Very little reference is given to the influence of education on the cultivation of creative potential for reasons of human development and satisfaction in living. If the public mind can be led to believe in the importance of the "creative class" to profit in the marketplace and as an influence on society, then certainly public opinion can become an active player in greater academic attention to the understanding of human potential for creative expression and positive change in the quality of thinking and the quality of a creative life.

The academics of creative education began some fifty years ago when J. P. Guilford, then president of the American Psychological Association, presented his Guilford Model of the Structure of Intellect to the 1950 annual conference. His three-dimensional theory defined an entire scope of human intellectual potential (see figure 3.1). One dimension dealt with five different possible contents of the mind, another with a variety of five mental processing operations of the content, and another with six possible products of that processing.

Altogether, his model identifies 150 distinct uses of the intellect (Guilford 1977). In the case of the products dimension, he proposed a hierarchy of levels of complexity of thought that serves as a guide to higher-order thinking. His model reminds us that instead of asking the IQ question, "How smart are you?" we can begin to ask, "How are *you* smart?" Almost everyone has some kind of special aptitudes or "smarts."

The feature of the Guilford Model that set up the discipline of creative studies as a focus of attention was the inclusion of divergent thinking in the listing of possible mental operations, a ranking newcomer to the traditional list. For the first time, divergent (creative) thinking took its place in equal status beside cognition, memory, convergent (right-answer), and evaluative thinking as an actual and potential capacity of the human mind. The immediate result was the activation of professional educators from fields of educational psychology, cognition, and human behavior in the investigation and research of creativity.

Outstanding among those educators identified early on with the discipline of creativity was E. Paul Torrance, whose lifetime leadership in the discipline of creativity included directorship of the Bureau of Educational Research at the University of Minnesota from 1958 to 1966. It was during those years that he developed the Minnesota Tests of Creative Thinking, which later became the Torrance Tests of Creative Thinking (Scholastic Testing Service 1980) and marked him from the beginning as the principal pioneer in the investigation and development of creative potential in students of all ages. His lifetime of service in the research and promotion of creative education is recorded in his biography, *E. Paul Torrance: The Creativity Man*, by Garnet Millar (1995). The enduring devotion of his students all over the world was expressed in a statement by Aurora Roldan in 1992: "The name E. Paul Torrance will forever be synonymous with creativity research. But for those of us who have been privileged to know him personally, his name is also synonymous with the concern, humility,

150 Ways to Use Your Brain

The Structure of Intellect

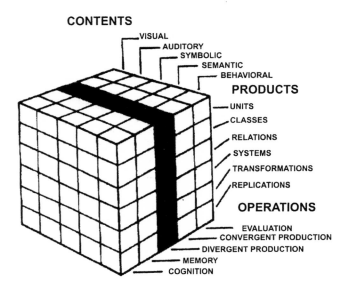

CONTENTS

VISUAL
AUDITORY
SYMBOLIC
SEMANTIC
BEHAVIORAL

PRODUCTS

UNITS
CLASSES
RELATIONS
SYSTEMS
TRANSFORMATIONS
REPLICATIONS

OPERATIONS

EVALUATION
CONVERGENT PRODUCTION
DIVERGENT PRODUCTION
MEMORY
COGNITION

Guilford, J.P. , Way Beyond the I.Q, 1977
Creative Education Foundation, Inc.
437 Franklin, Buffalo, N.Y. 14202

Products of Thought = A Hierarchy

Low Complexity: **UNITS** – Single Thing
CLASSES – Label – Categorize
RELATIONS – Sameness – differences – Cause and Effect
SYSTEMS – Holistic – Interactive realities (environment)
TRANSFORMATIONS – Creating and responding to Change
High Complexity: **IMPLICATIONS** –Some time reality in the future

Figure 3.1.   Guilford Model of the Structure of the Intellect.

and generosity which are the marks of a truly great man. It's no wonder that he is so well loved!" (Millar 1995, xiv).

Another educator who contributed significantly to the beginning of academic attention to creativity is Donald MacKinnon, director of the Institute for Personality Assessment and Research at the University of

California at Berkeley during the early academic attention to creativity. His research on intellectual development and personal effectiveness set guidelines for the understanding of qualities and recognizable features of the creative personality (MacKinnon 1978, 73–75).

John Curtis Gowan (1975) added further reaches of the human mind to studies of creativity. His perceptions and investigations of human consciousness and intellectual potential opened new doors of understanding and connected the realities of superconsciousness to issues of creative potential.

These four educators remain for me the principal architects of the educational discipline of creativity in its most comprehensive scope. They were present at the annual Creative Problem Solving Institutes sponsored by the Creative Education Foundation in Buffalo, New York, when I began my series of almost forty annual pilgrimages to Buffalo in June 1964 for the annual institute. It was there that I expanded and fortified my compelling interest in creativity and its importance to education. Because of Torrance's initiatives in studies of creativity in my educational community, and of my early identification with his work, my opportunities for leadership in the emerging field of creative studies followed quite naturally.

The satisfaction of introducing students, the educational community, and the interested public to the discovery and activation of their creative brain was immense. Practicing the art of creative problem solving individually and in groups was a stimulating and practical exercise. For forty years, I watched participants in university classes, business seminars, and workshops respond with enthusiasm to the creative thinking and problem-solving activities and to the theoretical base of the discipline. At Metropolitan State University and the University of St. Thomas in St. Paul and Minneapolis, Minnesota, I designed courses in creative studies and futures studies for graduate education and business/entrepreneurship departments.

The response was so enthusiastic that I established the University of St. Thomas Center (later Institute) for Creative Studies that served community interest by offering seminars, conferences, workshops, and certificate programs for the general public. The service was, for the most part, offered on a volunteer basis with the able support of work-study students and community volunteers. Outstanding among that population was the most valuable service of Steve Dahlberg, who began as a work-study student, became a colleague, and is presently director of the Creative Education Foundation in Buffalo.

One more personal observation on education: My early teaching experiences in a rural school and in a small Minnesota town had created an overwhelming interest in observations of student diversities and aptitudes. Intuitively, I became a student-oriented educator with ideas about individual potential and motivation. The common need of students for personal identity and recognition, the sense of significance, and the urge for self-expression were constantly evident. When I resumed my education much later at the University of Minnesota in 1966, a class with Dr. Torrance introduced me to the discipline of creative studies. The effect was like a thunderbolt. My intuitions about students became educationally justified and authentic. I had found my professional home in the field of creativity.

There is no doubt that when people interested in educational programming become aware of the reasons for identifying and exercising the creativity force in everyone, there will be public support for more official attention to creative education. The accumulation of studies and resources provides a clear message of the importance of creative expression in personal lives and of new and creative ways of thinking in the arena of human affairs. The discipline of creativity is not a trivial accompaniment to education. It is an authentic, serious matter for serious leadership for all ages of people and for the age of global transition, which cries out for new ways of thinking, in which the human family has to be engaged. As Torrance often said, "Creativity is too important to be left to chance."

Some progress has been made in educational attention to the creativity factor. Programs in teacher education departments began to add creativity to classes for gifted children after Torrance's work showed that identifying giftedness only on the basis of IQ tests missed a high percentage of the creatively gifted. His leadership in broadening the concept of giftedness brought the identification and practice of creative talent into focus for the special field of gifted education. That brought creative education into the lives of selected students; some creative teaching found its way into regular classes, but there was no guarantee of an automatic transfer of creative thinking activities to all students. Certainly, with the present federal reliance on standardized testing for the assessment of learning in the No Child Left Behind mandate, creative teaching is increasingly left to chance.

Current authorities like Howard Gardner (1993) and Robert Sternberg (2003) continue to update perceptions of creative intelligence in academic circles. Their work is taking a broader look at seven identified human intelligences (Gardner 1993). Sternberg (2003) has recently argued for a new set of "Three R's"—reasoning, resilience, and responsibility—as fundamental to successful intelligence. Their work has caught the attention of academics and scholars. What is more desperately needed is a shift of focus from research and testing to a broader application of actual teaching strategies that stimulate interest in a creative use of the mind as a motivator to the learning of content (Swartz and Parks 1994).

The best way to make use of the work of the pioneers of creativity is to concentrate on the integration of theory and application that they did so well. For too long, there has been a separation between theoretical understandings that answer to *Why?* and the so-called commonsense application that focuses on the *What*. Departments of educational psychology in higher education need to continue to include the theoretical background of the discipline of creativity at the same time that teacher education–methods courses need to practice the art of creative teaching with a clear understanding of the reasons for theoretical applications. A greater integration of learning and thinking in the processes of education is long overdue.

The entrenched habits of thinking in the establishment have a history of defending against efforts for educational reform. The bureaucratic fortress of tradition discourages the most energetic arguments for updating public education. The current directive of the federal government for educational programming is a prime example of the abuse of power to interfere with educational objectives. The overwhelming burden of mandated standardized testing at the expense of student growth and development in thinking beyond the level of facts and predetermined right answers is simplistic. Enlightened teachers, administrators, and general public have been raising objections to the focus on tests, measurements, and computerized statistics as the standard guide for assessing learning. They believe that knowledge and information are an important means, but the end objective of schooling goes beyond numbers. Jean Piaget said it well:

> The principal goal of education is to create men and women who are capable of doing new things, not simply of repeating what other generations have done . . . men and women who are creative, inventive discoverers. The second goal of education is to form minds which can be critical, can verify and not accept everything they are offered. (10)

Habits of thought in a culture are the result of a number of influences during the early years. One of those influences is formal education. Everyone is required to attend school for at least twelve years in this country; it is the law. The intellectual and social experiences of students during those years in school in the company of their peers have a powerful effect on an individual's preparation for a satisfying life in a dynamically changing world. Acquiring knowledge and information is important. So also are the influences of affective factors, such as personal value systems, positive self-concepts, creative problem-solving skills, capacities for higher-order thinking, responsibility, empathy for differences, talents for teamwork, independent judgment, and whatever else contributes to effective, engaged citizenship.

It has been said that almost everything we do is affected by our habits of thought. School is a natural place for the cultivation of creative, complex mental habits. Creative class activities that invite and practice independent thinking foster confidence and involvement of students. Teacher education courses need to equip teachers with skills for teaching course content through creative exercise of the mind. Enlightened teachers do it well as an automatic practice of their profession. All teachers need to be well schooled in the art. A teacher's observation from a book on *Creative Teaching and Learning* (Fryer 1996) suggested that most teachers believe that creativity is important, but they don't feel that they know very much about how to teach it.

There is another purpose in offering opportunities in schooling that demonstrate the higher-order thinking already present in many students. The right to express oneself, to think and be heard—these human rights can be protected in any classroom. Creative expression in the graphic arts, in writing, music, and dance is familiar. Creative thinking applied to science and discovery, mechanics, symbolism, leadership, problem solving, philosophical discourse, and so forth can also be evoked in school experiences. Teachers of excellence and insight who go beyond the established curricula are likely to recognize special creative-thinking talents in students and provide opportunities for their recognition and reward. Such teachers will be the ones who will be remembered for a student's lifetime, with gratitude for their mentoring.

The attitudes and behaviors of highly creative personalities often cause a separation between students and their peers, as well as estrangement with the daily menu of standardized programs. Early studies of creativity resulted in a list of qualities that identify highly creative personalities (MacKinnon 1978). MacKinnon's list of traits is based on research studies of creative architects, and is provided here for the reader's information. An understanding of behavioral traits of highly creative persons has application to the general population and often, in a very significant way, to children and young adults.

TRAITS OF HIGHLY CREATIVE PEOPLE

- Originality. Originality and creativity of thinking and in approaches to problems; constructive ingenuity; ability to set aside established conventions and procedures where appropriate.
- Esthetic sensitivity. A deep-seated preference for an appreciation of elegance of form and of thought, of harmony wrought from complexity, and of style as a medium of expression.
- Sense of destiny. This includes something of resoluteness and egotism, but over and above these, a belief in the foregone certainty of the worth and validity of one's attainments and future.
- Ideational responsiveness. Stimulated by the ideas and remarks of others, sensitive to the implications of what others say, and readily follows up.
- Cognitive flexibility. The ability to restructure, to shift and to adapt, and to deal with the new, the unexpected, and the unforeseen.
- Independence. Not bound by the conventions of most people; seeks independence in thought, manner, activity, and belief; sees himself or herself as free of the petty concerns and constraints of the ordinary person.
- Inquiringness as a habit of mind. An unending curiosity about things, about people, and about nature; an inner spur toward resolutions and discernment.
- Sense of personal identity. Self-insight and self-acceptance; an authentic, deeply rooted, socially responsible individual, which is expressed in most significant interactions.
- Intellectual competence. Effective utilization of the capacity to think, to reason, to comprehend, and to know.
- Cathexis of intellectual activity. Values cognitive pursuits, likes to think, analyze and understand; seeks out intellectually stimulating situations; enjoys tasks that demand intellectual effort for solution.
- Critical judgment. Good insight concerning ideas; able to see to the heart of the matter; seldom wrong in decisions about the relative merit of an idea.

- Social acuity. Observant and perceptive; quick to respond to the subtleties and nuances of others' behavior. (73–74)

Many readers will identify with a number of these traits and realize for the first time that they have characteristics that mark them as highly creative, even when they have "never done well in art." Many will begin to understand why their school experiences in a traditional, standardized system of learning seemed a misfit for their interests.

Years of academic studies and research have created a storehouse of information that can provide a wealth of understanding of creative talents and potential. The Torrance Tests of Creative Thinking (Scholastic Testing Service 1966) are available for the identification of creative potential in children as young as kindergarten age. Torrance's contributions to the discovery and development of creativity in children and adults is unparalleled. His life work has been thoroughly and lovingly recorded by his student and colleague in the biography, *E. Paul Torrance: The Creativity Man* (Millar 1995).

This period of radical change in personal, social, and world affairs challenges the human mind. New ideas and new ways of thinking are more critical to human society and to our institutions than they have ever been. Isn't it logical that everyone who is concerned with the quality of life on planet Earth would want creative and other complex thinking processes to be specifically taught to everyone during the years of formal education? Isn't it too late for "education as usual"?

Schools pay an abundance of attention to what students know. Shouldn't they be paying as much attention to how students use what they know, and shouldn't we be asking the ultimate question: "Are students including service to the community and to the common good in the use of their education?"

4

HABITS OF THOUGHT

There are one-story intellects, two-story intellects, and three-story intellects with skylights. All fact-collectors who have no aim beyond their facts are one-story men. Two-story men compare, reason, generalize, using the labor of the fact-collectors as their own. Three-story men idealize, imagine, predict, their best illumination comes from above through the skylight.

—Oliver Wendell Holmes

It has been said that we have changed everything in the world except the way we think. Since every important thing we do is affected by our habits of mind, there is a serious need to update those habits. It can be done. Higher order thinking can be deliberately taught, and it can be taught within the context of established curricula. The time has come for educationists to get serious about raising the level of thinking as a declared purpose of formal schooling.

School and society have always been acknowledged to be interdependent. Certainly radical changes like the arrival of the Information Age, the global society, scientific developments, and electronic communication systems have created a new kind of complex world that demands more complex thinking on the part of leadership and everyone else. Skills of creative and critical thinking, problem solving, and conflict resolution have become prerequisites for meeting new lifetime challenges not covered in the textbook or in the teacher's notes. What is required is independent thinking at new, more multifaceted levels.

Changing old habits is a daunting task—ask any golfer who is trying to improve his game by changing his swing. It requires new understanding of fundamentals, a lot of practice, and the will to change. If educational systems really want to prepare students to function effectively and productively in a democratic, rapidly changing world and/or workplace, they will have to add to their curricula the specific teaching of thinking processes. They will teach the metacognitive skills that give students an understanding of their own thinking and learning styles along with plenty of practice in the art of complex thinking. They will provide a learning climate that invites the discovery of student potential to think globally, futuristically, and with a talent for recognizing the systemic, interactive nature of all organizations.

The time-honored Model of the Structure of Intellect (see figure 3.1) introduced by J. P. Guilford fifty years ago (1968, 1977) is the best way to understand levels of complexity in the ways we think. On the products dimension of his model, he lists six levels of thought, arranged hierarchically in an ascending order with the least complex at the bottom of the list:

6. Thinking in Implications (with vision and some time reality in the future)
5. Thinking in Transformations (creating ideas and implementing positive change)
4. Thinking in Systems (having perceptions of the interconnected total operating system)
3. Thinking in Relationships (recognizing differences, sameness, cause/effect realities)
2. Thinking in Classes (categorizing, labeling, counting, grouping people and things)
1. Thinking in Units (Perceiving a single item unrelated to any system)

It is important to remember that any one of the six products could relate to any number of contents, including graphic arts, music, writing, architecture, symbols, behavior, leadership, and so on. The content items are not arranged in a hierarchy on the model.

The increasing complexity of products of thought that move from number 1 (units) to number 6 (implications) is easily recognizable. The number 2 level, thinking in classes, is a dominant feature of our culture. Categorization by age, by income, by level of formal education, by culture, by religion, by political preference, and so forth are basic to the organization of society. The problem is the tendency to become so absolute about the label that the singularity and uniqueness of persons or other classified subjects can be ignored or lost.

Especially in the practice of educational classifications of students by culture, economics, IQ scores, achievement records, attention deficit disorders, or any other such category, the label becomes so strong an influence that the unique nature and potential of the student can become lost, and expectations for student achievement distorted. Classification for the purposes of organization serves human differences more effectively when accompanied by flexible and sensitive habits of thought with practice in the systemic level of thinking.

The tendency to operate at the mental level of classes defines much of the thinking throughout society. New acquaintances are readily labeled according to where they live, the kind of car they drive, what kind of work they do, where they go to church, how they vote, their level of formal education, and more. Such standardization gets in the way of understanding a person as a unique, special human system. Sometimes the person himself stops at the classification level of thought and regards himself as a permanently labeled class of citizen. The tendency to think at a level of classes denies the more complex identity of a person as a growing, evolving human system within the larger system of society who has the power to change as a person and to contribute to the human, global systems of which he is a part.

Habits of thought in a society can hypnotize a culture into continuing to behave in the same old familiar comfort zone based on the same old belief systems of other generations. There comes a time, however, when some members of society recognize the challenges of the changing scene and the critical need for new patterns of thought that extend beyond the limitation of old habits. The advanced level of their intellectual vitality and mentality causes them to embrace perceptions of the total, interactive system and predict visions of a better future. There has never been a time when the complexity of world affairs demanded new, more complex ways of thinking by both leadership and followership. Creating a voting population with quality thinking habits is a logical and immediate addition to the purposes of educational systems everywhere.

The old habits of dualistic thinking are a result of thinking in classes and labels, and they continue to severely limit social progress. Positioning ourselves with a label that reflects one or the other side of a dichotomy creates a stranglehold on our thinking and accomplishes nothing more than high-grade competition. Liberal or conservative, privileged or poor, Democrat or Republican, with us or against us, Christian or non-Christian, beautiful or ugly—any two pairs of opposites may provide the comfort of like-minded company, but they exert a public control over any kind of enlightenment and any hope for a peaceful resolution of differences (Kaufmann 1970).

So if educational systems really want to prepare students to function effectively and productively in a democratic, rapidly changing world and/or workplace, they will have to add the specific teaching of thinking processes to their curricula. They will teach the metacognitive skills that give students an understanding of their own thinking and learning styles along with plenty of practice in the art of thinking creatively, critically, and in problem-solving modes. They will provide a learning climate that invites the discovery of student potential to think globally, futuristically, and with a talent to think beyond the level of categories and classifications to the higher order, quality mental processes.

That kind of intelligence requires the practice of deliberately thinking about thinking, a new trend among serious students and scholars who wonder about our time and its unique place in human history. The current world zeitgeist demands intellects capable of absorbing untold quantities of new information and processing the whole collection with imagination, vision, and an awareness of the realities. The challenges of living together harmoniously with all of the diversities intact are within our reach. Educational programs and human development training can confront the challenge of improving the quality of thinking for every citizen.

The recent introduction of the concept of spiral dynamics to human discourse is stimulating thought and discussion about levels of human consciousness closely related to the ideas on levels of thought according to the Guilford Model. Don Beck, founder and president of the Institute for Values and Culture, is also CEO of the Spiral Dynamics Global Group and a leading authority on spiral dynamics. He is "a global visionary who is increasingly being heard in international forums and high levels of governmental leadership around the world" (Arlington Institute, 60).

The concept of spiral dynamics represents human thought and consciousness in eight levels of development, from fundamental to universal. A system developed by Scott, Brennecke, and Engelsen (2003) provides a brief representation of the eight levels of consciousness, ascending in complexity, in the following order:

- Instinct and Survival
- Magic and Mysticism
- Ego and Self-Development
- Meaning and Order
- Autonomy and Achievement
- Community and Compassion
- Integration and Systems
- Universal and Holistic

Symptoms of a growing awareness and interest in the public mind of the integration of the sciences and humanities in the universal order include the enthusiastic public response to the recent philosophically provocative film, *What the Bleep Do We Know?* Anyone familiar with the early writing of the French scientist/philosopher, Teilhard de Chardin in *The Phenomenon of Man* (1966) will be reminded of his ideas.

The government alone cannot address the problems of society. Money alone cannot reinvent education. Traditional habits of educational leadership and teaching skills are inadequate for the task of educating human minds for maximum performance. In a democracy where adult citizens who have the power and privilege of a vote, what is needed is a mentality that has learned to think independently at the highest possible level. Buckminster Fuller gave us a sample of his own thinking when he said that "If humanity is to pass safely through the present crisis on earth, it will be because a majority of individuals are now doing their own thinking" (Gelb 1995, xxiv).

There is no quick fix for the challenge of educational reform. The habits of perceiving education as a process of transferring an accumulation of knowledge and skills from an authority to a learner in competition for a grade with other learners have begun to change, but not fast enough. Habits of administration based on a system resembling the military "chain of command" fail to capitalize on the insights and new ideas of educators at lower levels of authority. Teachers and administrators of excellence often have little confidence that their innovative ideas for improving education will be given a serious hearing and consideration by decision makers in the system. It would be helpful if the old habits of top-down management of education could give way to a more inclusive leadership that would make good use of the powerful thinking resources at the lower levels of authority available in most schools.

It would be a good thing if all educational bureaucrats could understand the importance of the deliberate teaching of some of the complex thinking strategies that are having increasing attention in classrooms at all levels. The practice of mind mapping (see appendix A) or cognitive mapping (sometimes called clustering) has been somewhat familiar in school activities from elementary levels all the way through college and universities. Mind mapping offers the opportunity to communicate the quality of thinking that records connections and relationships to a central theme in an open-ended, right-brained system or map (Buzan and Buzan 1993).

When I introduced the concept of mind mapping in an MA program in teacher education some time ago, I was impressed with later reports from teachers who had made use of the teaching strategy in their elementary school classes. In every case, the results with children had the effect of identifying students whose natural systemic thinking style responded enthusiastically to the process. Many students whose written work had been half-hearted became motivated to record their systemic thinking patterns by means of symbols and a minimum of words.

Michael Gelb (1998), in his book on *How to Think Like Leonardo da Vinci*, provided guidelines and simple rules for mind mapping:

- Be prepared with a topic to think about, a few colored pencils, and a large sheet of paper.

- Begin your mind map with a symbol or a picture representing your topic at the center of your page.
- Write down key words of recall and creative association.
- Connect the key words with lines radiating from your central image.
- Print the key words. Limit the number of words per line.
- Use colors, pictures, dimension, and codes for greater association and emphasis.
- Be original in developing a map that does the best job of communicating your thinking about the topic.

Once the habit of mind mapping is established, it can become a useful tool when planning an event, developing a report, taking notes, reviewing for a test, creating change, and any other communication system for including the interconnected parts or concepts of a topic. Mind mapping helps to avoid tunnel vision and create awareness of the interconnectedness of all things and phenomena. Mind mapping elevates the level of thinking in complex systems.

Discovering and practicing the art of systemic thinking by mind mapping should be an essential part of the school program. Many teachers are familiar with its stimulating influence on learning when associated with the teaching of content.

Now let's look at strategies for exercising the complex thinking capacities to visualize and to speculate on possible futures and implications of observable trends. The World Future Society has been leading the way for the activation of mental processes that identify trends in society or organizations and for speculating on the possible results of the continuation of the trend in the years ahead. The advantage for planners is that if the predictable future of the trend is perceived to be negative, interventions can be made to derail possible future problems and deal with them while still in their beginning stages. Exercising the mental muscle for complex thinking in future time prepares the population and its leaders for long-range, wise decision making. Problems that arise from simplistic thinking and impulsive action, so costly to government, can be avoided.

A simple exercise in shaking up the implications level of thinking has its base in the question, "What might be the result if . . . ?" Teachers of any class level can design the question to reflect the content of a lesson or a response to a news report. Students or participants are invited to be both imaginative and practical in their speculations about alternative possibilities of the future where they will be spending the rest of their lives. For example:

"What might be the result in five years if the price of gasoline continues to increase?"

"What might be the effect on education and society ten years from now if distance learning and independent study continue to expand?"

One of the best examples of programs for the development of visionary thinking was created by Torrance as early as 1974, in the form of the Future Problem Solving Program. There were two major purposes for the program: (1) to help schools do more to assist students in developing their creative-thinking talents, and (2) to help students focus on the future that they would encounter as they entered adulthood. Using the creative problem-solving process designed by Alex Osborn (1953) for business and industry, students worked in teams of four to identify future world problems and generate original ideas for possible solutions. Within ten years, the project had developed into a year-long curriculum reaching approximately 175,000 students all over the world (Hester 1994, 43). It would be a boon to efforts for new, more complex habits of thinking in the world if programs of this kind could become mandated by educational leadership everywhere.

Many teachers and administrators of excellence have already changed their habits of educating. In spite of the prescriptive nature of central authority and standardized programs, they have found ways to update and enhance the school program to include activities that provide students the freedom to think and be heard at the same time that they allow themselves the freedom to teach and administer. Educators of intellect and humanistic judgment can provide models for new habits of educating if the system will be flexible enough to grant them the freedom to think and be heard in the "Halls of Ivy."

A new educational plan modeled by a small-town teacher in Minnesota (John Davis) is bringing complex thinking into focus for students from all over the country. He created the Great American Think-Off, a debate competition designed to promote complex thinking and make philosophy "fun and accessible for the average person." As a spin-off to the Think-Off, he created the Kids Philosophy Slam for students in kindergarten through high school. The first question was, "Which is more powerful, love or hate?" A subsequent question was, "What is the meaning of life?" There were more than 125,000 responses (*Minneapolis Star Tribune*, April 25, 2003, p. B9). Entries were judged and prizes awarded.

My conversations with a cross section of the population, including parents, professional educators, school board members, retired teachers, the business community, and opinionated citizens of diverse backgrounds, reveal a new awareness of the importance of educational reform and a new recognition of the role of the people as co-creators of the culture. There is evidence that new ways of thinking are emerging in the public mind, both inside and outside of positions of authority. This passage from a current but unidentified piece of writing in my files deserves to be incorporated:

> The originality of our time is that attention is turning away from conflict to information. The new ambition is to prevent disasters, illnesses and crimes before they occur and to treat the globe as a single whole; women's entry into the public sphere is reinforcing the challenge to the tradition that conquest is the supreme goal of existence; more attention is being given to understanding other people's emotions than to making and unmaking institutions. Yet much of what people do is governed by old ways of thinking. Both politics and economics [add education] have been powerless in the face of the obstinacy of entrenched mentalities. Mentalities cannot be changed by decree because they are based on memories, which are almost impossible to kill. But it is possible to expand one's memories by expanding one's horizons, and when that happens there is less chance that one will go on playing the same old tunes for ever and repeating the same mistakes.

Unless institutions of education continue to make changes in their way of educating, society will go on playing the same old tunes. Unless students are deliberately helped to understand the higher order thinking patterns available to them and to practice the art of serious, complex thinking, old habits of thought will continue to dominate their personal and professional lives as well as the future of society and maybe even the survival of the planet.

The job of changing habits of thought is not about the incidental assignments that challenge the thinking of students beyond memory, cognition, and arriving at a predetermined, right answer. It is about the specific teaching and cultivation of the brain's higher power to think independently at levels of critical, creative, visionary, transformational, and systemic thought. Courses in educational psychology that include studies of thought processes need to become a part of every academic discipline. Every student needs to understand the integrative nature of all of learning and the interdependency of life on the "little blue planet" that we call Earth.

Serious attention to the art of thinking is not a new idea. An old book with the title *The Art of Thinking* found its way some time ago from an old book shop to my collection. Authored by Ernest Dimnet, a French writer, and published in 1928 by Simon and Schuster, the gentle wisdom of the book is prophetic in some ways of the current state of the individual in society and of an educational system that fails to develop each individual's capacity for higher order, independent thinking and personal identity. An observation in the book on the issue of sports in schools as early as 1928 would have interest for those who feel the attention to sports is excessive.

> The predominance of sports in schools, in the national life, in the press, not only crowds out what is or should be more important, but it creates an atmosphere in which these important things are made to appear superfluous, or are even described in extremely disrespectful slang. What does seem important is a bustling, hustling life, with the excitement of getting in or out of a scrimmage, beating somebody or something, getting there. All of which is, within its limits, an excellent way of looking at life, but it is not culture. Thoughtfulness, which is the highest form of life, is reconcilable with tussle only in a deep biological sense which is too subtle for this practical book to enter into. The plain fact is that the boy who shows the greatest activity or initiative on the game field is not by any means always the one who asks the most intelligent questions. (67)

Democracies have always known that they depend upon the voice of an informed public if they are to function effectively. The dynamically changing and complex global nature of society has to add a new requirement to the traditional qualification of informed citizens. Now the voting public needs to exercise habits of thinking that can process the overwhelming quantities of information and arrive at independent opinions on issues vital to the country.

It is too simplistic to continue to depend upon a party label or the blind adherence to old lines of thought left over from other generations when exercising the privilege of voting. What is desperately needed is a paradigm shift to new, more complex ways of thinking, and the school is the logical place for the learning to be delivered. It can be done. It is being done in selected places. What is needed is a general movement that will urge for opening the doors of educational policy beyond money and numbers to the development of the most unlimited resource in all of society—the human mind.

⑤

E. PAUL TORRANCE AND HIS CREATIVE EDUCATION LEGACY: SELF-EXPRESSION IS THE PRIMARY SACRAMENT OF THE UNIVERSE

Don't waste a lot of expensive, unproductive energy in trying to be well-rounded. Learn the skills of interdependence, giving freely from the infinity of your greatest strengths.

—E. Paul Torrance

No one in all the fifty-year history of the development of the academic discipline of creative education has been a more tireless pioneer, authentic researcher, dedicated teacher, good friend, and mentor than Dr. E. Paul Torrance, "Creativity Man." His death, in 2003, deprived the world of a true champion and spokesman for the nature and nurture of the creative spark in everyone. Students and colleagues from all over the world express profound appreciation for his work.

From Nava Butler-Por, Haifa, Israel: His unique contribution to our understanding of the creative spirit and the processes by which they can be developed in children of all cultures is universal and has benefited scientists, educators, children and parents all over the world. (Millar 2004, 15)

From Aurora Roldan, Manila, Philippines: The name E. Paul Torrance will forever be synonymous with creativity research. But for those of us who have been privileged to know him personally, his name is also synonymous with the concern, humility, and generosity which are the marks of a truly great man. It's no wonder that he is so well loved! (Millar 2004, 14)

Everyone interested in the education of children and youth is entitled to know about the contributions of Torrance to the identification and development of their special talents. Higher education, especially teacher education programs, need to vigorously promote, authorize, and require a thorough background in the discipline of creativity for everyone who will be spending time in a position of influence in the company of children and young people. Parents and all the rest of society will be more effective in their efforts to influence the educational groundwork for life and learning if they have an understanding of the meaning of creativity according to Torrance.

I have every reason to want to bring his message to public attention. It was his work and his support that made possible my career as an educational entrepreneur in creative studies and futures studies. His influence began when I was a fifty-eight-year-old undergraduate student at the University of Minnesota, where Torrance was already an established authority on creativity. Many other grateful and devoted Torrance students are carrying on his leadership all over the world.

In spite of the serious scholarship that has produced an academic discipline of creative studies and in spite of the dramatic changes in the lives and spirit of students who engage in programs of creative development, society continues to have a limited understanding of creativity. Say the word in most groups of citizens, and the first response will be a connection to the arts. That is certainly a valid connection. It is also a very limited one.

Current official statements of educational purposes frequently include a reference to the teaching of critical thinking. The growing public acknowledgment that government needs to operate with more imagination calls serious attention to the fact that mandated curriculum and learning standards from centers of educational central authority need to begin including creative thinking in teaching requirements.

The fact that the discipline of creative education has been relatively neglected in official standards may be part of the reason that most of the general public is quick to appreciate creativity in the arts, but has little understanding of the scope and scholarship of studies of creativity as related to quality thinking, to human potential, to human behavior, to self-esteem and achievement, and actually to a full and satisfying life—and even beyond that to a better society, a global perspective, and peace in the world.

Seminars on creative problem solving in the public domain can have resounding effects on personal habits of thought. The academic level of creative studies has a more comprehensive purpose. As an important component of departments of educational psychology, it includes qualitative and quantitative research, academic reports and reviews, resources for teachers, and the practical integration of creative studies with cognition, psychology, philosophy, global studies, leadership, environmental studies, scientific investigation, and the arts of writing, graphics, theater, music, and every other study that opens the mind to higher-order thinking in behalf of personal development, public service, and everything in between.

Torrance's research and inquiry went way beyond the obvious connections between studies of creativity and studies of a wide range of human behavior. The listing of his published writing in his biography (Millar 1995) is testimony to his vigorous pursuit of understanding of the role of creative expression in the forming and transforming of a personality. The records show 9,785 published articles, books, reviews, and miscellaneous papers with titles relating the human factor of creativity to a wide diversity of human development. Here is a sampling of titles:

- Some Implications of Creativity Research for Gifted Education
- International Bibliography on Stimulating Creativity
- Future Problem-Solving and Quality Circles in Schools
- The Mandate: A New Image of Teaching
- The Importance of Falling in Love with Something
- America's Energy Is Mindpower
- Children of the World: Hopeful but Worried
- Creativity in Communications
- Implications of Whole-Brained Theories of Learning and Thinking
- Testing the Creativity of Preschool Children
- Tests of Creative Thinking Scoring Guide
- Misconceptions about Creativity in Gifted Children: Removing the Limits on Learning

- What Happens When Children Study the Future?
- Status of Creative Women
- The Role of Mentors in Creative Achievement
- Meeting the Needs of Creatively Gifted Children
- Creativity and a Changing View of Teaching
- How Parents Might Help Gifted Children Maintain Their Creativity
- Conditions for Invention and Innovation
- Creative Retirement Provides a Fair Chance to Grow
- A Change in Concepts of Intelligence
- Intense Emotional Experience: Impetus to Creation
- Save Tomorrow for the Children
- A Reaction to Gifted Black Students: Curriculum and Teaching Strategies
- Creativity and Teaching Concepts of God
- On the Shoulders of Giants: What Humans Can Become
- Beyonders and Their Characteristics
- Maintaining Creativity in Later Years
- Why Fly? A Philosophy of Creativity
- High Tech, Aesthetics, Art and Art Education
- Growing Up Creatively Gifted with Learning Disabilities

The list is staggering. To those who didn't know the intensity of Torrance's devotion to service, it would seem an impossibility. Many of his written contributions were in response to the countless requests for his opinions and endorsements. Many were in collaboration with students who had some role in the development of a study or a research project. Torrance was the most generous of professors in acknowledging any contribution to his work. Having a graduate student's name appear with Torrance's was a mark of distinction. It may have been that because the Torrances had no children, they substituted students for the beneficiaries of their caregiving spirit. Hundreds of students and colleagues have fond memories of the constancy of support, encouragement, and mentoring that was always offered promptly and graciously. There will always be a grateful Torrance Fan Club in the world.

One of his most significant contributions for educators and anyone interested in discovering creative thinking talent was the development of the

Torrance Tests of Creative Thinking. They continue to be published by Scholastic Testing Service, Bensenville, Illinois, and have been translated for use in many other countries. Their arrival on the educational scene in the mid-sixties threw open the doors of perception regarding gifted children. The Torrance Tests made it possible to identify creatively talented children and to add them to the list of identified high-IQ students for advanced programming. It was a major breakthrough that broadened the old concept of giftedness to include the creatively talented.

One early difficulty in the use of the tests was the fact that the open-ended invitation to students for the cognitive factors of original, flexible, fluent, elaborative thinking made the scoring extremely complex and required specially trained scorers. My service as an aide in the Torrance office at the University of Minnesota came at a time when he had designed scoring directions for his tests that would give classroom teachers the skills to assess test results of their students with reliable accuracy. As a member of his staff, I became directly involved in the experiment with teacher scoring. At the time, my husband was an elementary school principal in the Minneapolis suburb of Richfield, Minnesota. His school had been chosen earlier by Torrance as an experimental site for research and demonstrations of creative teaching; I was privileged to serve as courier for testing materials back and forth between the Torrance office and Lincoln Hills School in Minnesota.

As a newcomer to the Torrance learning society, I felt an exciting personal relationship to the paper-and-pencil tests that called for students' imaginative responses to a number of different creative-thinking tasks. Later on, in my role of state consultant for gifted and talented in Minnesota and in my university teaching of courses in creative thinking, I designed a mock exercise of one of the figural tasks in the Torrance Test (see figure 5.1). Created as an adaptation, these provided examples of the cognitive factors of creative thought. A composite sample of adult responses to the Incomplete Figures Task is shown in figure 5.2. I made consistent use of the exercise as an experiential learning strategy for introducing students to the idea of independent, original expression of their own thinking. In addition, a review of the results helped to introduce me to the individual thinking styles of students

Parents and teachers who are acquainted with the Torrance Tests of Creative Thinking know how effective their use is in recognizing innate creative talents. Although the tests are based on creative expression through figural (drawing) and verbal modes, the tests offer clues to thought patterns that apply to all forms of creative production. A major advantage of reviewing a student's responses to the tasks is a better understanding of student interests and attitudes.

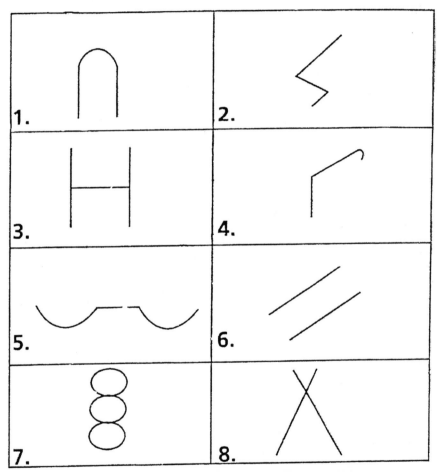

Figure 5.1. Creative thinking exercise for classroom use, adapted from Torrance Tests of Creative Thinking.
*Picture Completion
By adding lines to the incomplete figures on this page, you can sketch some interesting objects or pictures. Try to think of some picture or object that no one else will think of. Try to make it tell as complete and as interesting a story as you can by adding to and building up your idea. Make up an interesting title for each of your drawings and write it at the bottom of each block next to the number of the figure.

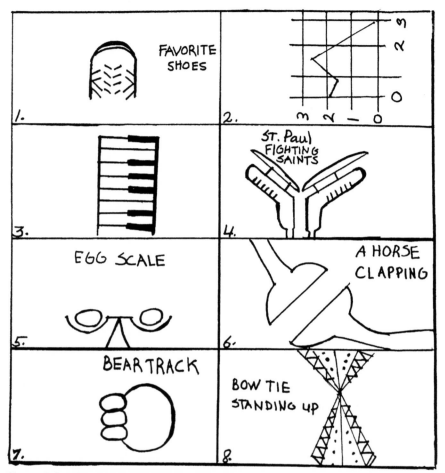

Figure 5.2. Examples of responses by students to exercise in creative expression adapted from Torrance Tests of Creative Thinking.

Torrance always spoke of his belief in the importance of creative thinking for students at every level from kindergarten through high school and beyond to adulthood.

First, it is important from the standpoint of personality development and mental health. I believe there is little question that prolonged, enforced repression of the creative desire may lead to actual breakdown of the personality. Its stifling cuts at the very roots of satisfaction in living and ultimately creates overwhelming tension.

Second, there seems to be little doubt that creative thinking contributes importantly to the acquisition of information, and may ultimately be demonstrated to be as important in this respect as memory and similar intellectual functions.

Third, creative thinking is certainly essential in the application of knowledge to daily personal and professional problems. For example, I have long contended that the reason courses in education and psychology have made no more difference than they have in the behavior of classroom teachers is that teachers have not been trained to use their imaginations in applying such knowledge.

Fourth, I believe it is tremendously important to society that our creative talent be identified, developed, and utilized. The future of our civilization depends upon the quality of the creative imagination of our next generation. Perhaps our need is not so much for more scientists and engineers but for more creative scientists and engineers. (Torrance 1995, 24)

Torrance's research and understanding regarding creative expression was consistently tied to a thorough knowledge of and empathy for victims of suppression of the creative spirit. He was concerned for the obedient, conforming child who may grow up with an uncertainty of confidence in his or her self-concept and who may have to depend upon someone else for making decisions. Also, special problems in schooling may have their source in the frustration of highly creative minds unable to deal with an extremely authoritarian learning climate. Learning disabilities, behavior problems, and juvenile delinquency have been found to be related to a consistent denial of the urge to create. It has been said that when people are deprived of the power of expression, they will express themselves in a drive for power.

Torrance believed that the art of responding creatively to stress was an important ingredient for dealing with troubling times (Torrance 1965). In 1986, he demonstrated his personal application of that art. The flight of the space shuttle *Challenger* was planned to be the flight for the common man, education, and human creativity. For the first time, a private citizen, teacher Christa McAuliffe, was chosen to represent the space program's universal purpose. Because June Scobee had studied with Torrance, and because she was the wife of shuttle commander Dick Scobee, an offer was made to Torrance to take some product of his research on the mission. He chose to send a set of the Torrance Tests of Creative Thinking. Because his tests had been translated into thirty-four languages, he felt they best represented a universal symbol for the teacher-in-space flight of the *Challenger*.

On the day of the flight, Torrance was watching the launch on television with all his understandable interest and pride when the ship unexpectedly exploded, killing all seven space travelers. He later reported the magnitude of the shock. He also reported that his response was a therapeutic writing of a poem descriptive of his feelings. He demonstrated a prime example of a creative response to stress. A personal characteristic that made his influence so powerful was the balance he brought to his store of knowledge and its application in his life. He was one of the best examples of what Harlan Cleveland has referred to as "a reflective practitioner and a practical academic."

Torrance was a lifelong champion and defender of creative teachers. His empathy for their nature and his appreciation for their accomplishments with students, especially those outside of the mainstream, appear with regularity in his lectures and writings. His observations deserve the serious attention of everyone who is concerned about the history of our failure to serve the educational needs of all children and to protect the status of all creative teachers. He wrote,

> Since creativity involves divergent (creative) thinking, we can expect the creative teacher to express ideas that differ from our own and from some of education's time-honored practices. Furthermore, since he cares naught for power, he is unlikely to change his thinking in order to curry favor with his superiors. He may be difficult to hold to routine and become restless under conventional restraint. He works best when dealing with difficult, challenging problems or when engrossed in a project that is his "baby." There will be times when he will defy precedent. He may try a new idea without official permission. (Torrance 1995, 14)

In his vision, the challenge of creative people in the workplace applies far beyond the classroom. He continues with the following hopefully prophetic statement:

> In time, our society will learn how to more effectively reward creativity in almost all fields of work. Today the creative worker everywhere can scarcely obtain rewards in proportion to his or her contribution without

accepting a position of power, an administrative job. Frequently, the demands of the administrative job spell the end of his making a creative contribution. We simply have to develop more satisfactory procedures for rewarding creative talent wherever it occurs. (Torrance 1995, 14)

Current publications like *The Cultural Creatives: How 50 Million People Are Changing the World* (Ray and Anderson 2000) and *The Rise of the Creative Class* (Florida 2002) are the beginning of public evidence that the wheels are turning in the direction of the Torrance vision. What is needed is the vigorous boost from public activists who "get the message" and keep their finger on the fast-forward button.

The lifetime contribution of Torrance to creative education always had the paradoxical quality of integrating two opposite perspectives at the same time. He relished the practical, hands-on time he spent in classrooms with children engaged in the creative expression of ideas, but he never lost track of the larger purpose of searching and making clear his insights into the relationship between creativity and the evolution of the human intellect. It was this mental capacity plus his dogged determination to move education ahead that makes him celebrated as the "Creativity Man" (Millar 1995).

Throughout Torrance's professional life, his inquisitive mind and his constant research, together with his continuing contacts with students, created a particular interest in creative people whose history and accomplishments set them apart as personalities that were "not afraid to take the creative leap beyond." He named them "Beyonders." Garnet Millar, former student and colleague of Torrance, is the author of *The Making of a Beyonder* (2004). His book reports Torrance's final research studies that revealed the most common characteristics of the Beyonder group (2004, v):

- a sense of mission in life
- love of one's work
- delight in deep thinking
- tolerance of mistakes
- not well-rounded
- comfortable as a minority of one
- courage to be creative

The book describes how individuals from the past, present, and future fit the characteristics of a Beyonder, as determined by the Torrance longitudinal research on creative individuals. Each chapter features accomplished figures—historical and contemporary—and offers activities, strategies, and tips to assist in the development of Beyonder characteristics for both leadership and followership in the years ahead (see appendix B, p. 131, for Beyonder Survey and Key).

The current state of uncertainty in world affairs is issuing a wake-up call to remind the present generation that they are responsible for the quality of life that will be inherited by future generations. Torrance, as usual, was way ahead in his thinking. In 1987, he collaborated with a group of colleagues to publish *Save Tomorrow for the Children* (Torrance 1987). The book features a collection of scenarios of the future written by children from ages nine to eighteen from all over the world. Scenario writing is a strategy that looks ahead to possible future results of current trends. If the scenario sees negative consequences of a trend, action may be taken to avoid the consequences predicted. The teaching of futures studies, as recommended by the World Future Society, includes classroom experiences in the writing of scenarios.

It is easy to claim Torrance to be a model of futuristic thinking at a level of implications on the Guilford Model of the Structure of Intellect (see figure 3.1). His writing marks him also with qualities of systemic thinking. His leadership saw the need for educational development of qualities of thinking throughout a participating population that serves the needs of a fully functioning democracy. His academic leadership provides a road map for not only cognitive intellectual evolution but also the development of attitudes and values at the highest human level. Authorities in the development of the affective domain describe the mature person as someone who

> extends his loyalties beyond himself and his immediate associates. He becomes devoted to such ideals as justice, liberty, tolerance, sympathy for the downtrodden, and other broad human values. He places these human values above personal gain, comfort and personal loyalties. A principle becomes more important than one's group, one's friends, even one's family. (Torrance 1965, 106)

There is nothing exaggerated about the claims made here for the value of Torrance's leadership in the search of more effective education in service to a free democratic society. As a Torrance scholar, I spent a minimum of time studying and defending the validity and reliability of his research. I left that part of the academic discipline to other professionals. I trusted the exceptional qualities of his mind and his genuinely spiritual values; I was happy to leave the analyses and numbers games to others. Actually, his research did not go unchallenged by academic proponents of the status quo. The Torrance work deserves high praise and dedicated "missionaries." He has left behind a multitude of educators prepared and eager to continue his lead. His legacy needs the understanding, support, and initiative of an informed public.

If I have personalized this chapter too much, I ask understanding from all the readers who have never experienced the gift of a creative teacher and mentor in their own lives. From those who have been so blessed, their understanding is automatically assured. I conclude this chapter with my "Manifesto on Creativity."

1. Society and its institutions are all at a breakpoint time in human history. Radical changes require new ways of thinking and operating in the workplace and throughout society.
2. The more complex an organization becomes, the more significant is each player.
3. Achieving the shared purpose of an organization or institution depends upon the fully functioning, creative talent of each individual.
4. Creative, critical thinking and innovative behavior are a present or potential talent in every human; new ways of thinking and behaving can be taught.
5. The discipline of creative studies, with its fifty years of development at the Creative Education Foundation in Buffalo, New York, is the international center of leadership and resources. Their Annual Creative Problem Solving Institute each June attracts, trains, and networks leaders in creativity from all over the world.
6. In spite of the explosion of literature and discussion on the importance of creativity and innovation, unless real, experiential, hands-on learning is provided, the nature of the creative process and spirit is not internalized and well practiced.

7. Talents for creating new ideas and managing new ideas are equally important to a learning organization.
8. Continuity and feedback in the practice of new ways of thinking are essential for personal and institutional change.
9. To be playful and serious at the same time is possible, and it defines the ideal mental condition. Creativity relates well to humor and good fun.

6

EDUCATION FOR
CREATIVE PROBLEM SOLVING

> The history of civilization is essentially the record of man's creative
> ability. Imagination is the cornerstone of human endeavor.
>
> —Alex Osborn

Many readers of this book will already have a profound acquaintance with the process of creative problem solving. For some, it will be a new and specific idea for meeting the educational and developmental needs of a diversity of students. Many readers will have been involved with the teaching and promotion of the experiential learning and mental exercises that introduce a participant to the reality of his or her creative potential. There is an excitement and lifelong value in discovering and exercising the gift of creative imagination in the solving of problems and the meeting of challenges. That learning process has been going on for more than fifty years, ever since Alex Osborn brought to public attention his ideas on *Applied Imagination* (Osborn 1953). The Osborn commitment to education was backed up by the establishment of the Creative Education Foundation, early in 1954, "solely for the purpose of encouraging a more creative trend in American education."

It wasn't long before Sidney Parnes joined with Osborn to create a structure for the teaching of the Osborn-Parnes Creative Problem Solving

Process, a system that has undergone few modifications since its initial design (Noller, Parnes, and Biondi 1976), and the tradition of the annual Creative Problem Solving Institute (CPSI) in Buffalo, New York, came into being. Sidney Parnes has carried the process forward for more than fifty years. In 2004, the fiftieth anniversary of the institute was celebrated in Buffalo, New York, with renewed energy and sense of purpose. Sometime during the fifty years, the original intention for service in creative education to American educational systems became internationalized. Participants from all over the world now attend and contribute to the annual institute.

A distinctive feature of the Osborn-Parnes Creative Problem Solving Process is its focus on experiential learning and thinking. Its best success depends upon the establishment of a learning climate of mutual trust, of freedom of ideation and its expression, and of overcoming the traditional constraints to imaginative thought. A particular value is practice in the higher-order, paradoxical art of being serious and playful at the same time.

There is something extremely individualistic about teaching creative problem solving. Any teacher or facilitator for a creative problem-solving experience will necessarily put his own interpretation on the open-ended nature of the process and make use of his own imagination to design learning and practice activities for the exercise of the mental muscle of creativity. There is, however, a solid basic structure and sequence for bringing a problem or challenge through a process that produces a creative/practical plan of action for its solution.

The Osborn-Parnes Creative Problem Solving Process has, along with personal creative development, a practical, futuristic purpose: "One cannot foresee exactly what knowledge will be needed five or ten years from now to meet life's problems. One can, however, develop attitudes and abilities that will help to meet any future challenge creatively by finding better solutions to problems (Noller, Parnes, and Biondi 1976). There have been a few minor modifications in the established procedure for the application of the Osborn-Parnes Creative Problem Solving Process. The original list of objectives of the program still applies:

1. An attitude of self-confidence in your ability to be deliberately creative.

2. A strong motivation to utilize your creative potential.
3. An open-mindedness to the ideas of others.
4. A greater expression of your curiosity—an awareness of the excitement and challenge in life.
5. A consciousness of the vital importance of creative effort in business, in the arts, in the professions, in scientific and technical pursuits, and in personal living.
6. A heightened sensitivity to the problems that surround you—an attitude of "constructive discontent" toward situations as they exist in your life (that is, a constant desire to improve everything that you do).
7. An increase in abilities associated with creativity, especially the ability to produce quality ideas and original ideas as leads to solutions of problems (Noller, Parnes, and Biondi 1976, 2).

Attendance for the first time at a Creative Problem Solving Institute sponsored by the Creative Education Foundation in Buffalo, New York, will lead to the discovery of genuine evidence that, at a Creative Problem Solving Institute, the stated objectives are in the process of being met. The sessions and general climate have an intensity of spirit and dynamic that is sustained for the entire scope of the program. Many of the institute leaders and participants return year after year to experience the stimulation and new learning for transfer back to their communities. The numbers attending have reached as high as eight hundred and more.

I was able to make almost forty annual visits to CPSI and transfer my experiences there to my career as an educational entrepreneur. The university courses in creative studies and problem solving that I designed and initiated for college and university programs gave me the pleasure of seeing students wake up to the power of their mind to think creatively in a higher education class and to have their ideas heard and valued. Especially in a required course in creative problem solving for a university entrepreneurship program, the application of the creative problem-solving process to a personal challenge often resulted in concrete solutions. The development and marketing of new, creative products was a frequent result of one of the course requirements; that is, to apply the problem-solving process to the identification of a recognized problem and create an invention that would solve the problem. Many of the course outcomes for students were less concrete or quantifiable. Statements from students in course evaluations at the end of the semester are evidence of the personal value of the learning experience (see appendix C).

There were times when I felt something of a critical attitude from other professors regarding the academic nature of the class in creative problem solving. That is probably true for educational entrepreneurs everywhere who introduce the experiential creative thinking and learning process to traditional academicians. In spite of the consistently strong student evaluations by the classes, and the praise and encouragement of the director of the entrepreneurship program, subtle references to the question of "academic rigor" from other professors were not infrequent. The nature of the course was unfamiliar enough to break with old habits and perceptions of college lecture-oriented classrooms.

At the beginning of the introduction of the course in a graduate education department, my departure from the traditional lecture arrangement of chairs in the classroom to the circle arrangement of chairs for group brainstorming teams was a hardship for the maintenance person. He ordered me to get the chairs back in straight rows where they belonged after class. Students were happy to comply. In time, suspicions were modified, and I began to hear from other professors that students from the problem-solving class were inclined to be major contributors to their class discussions and to produce more original and imaginative ideas in their writing assignments. Also, the arrangement of chairs in a pattern for class discussion became commonplace.

It is not too surprising that a wake-up experience in creative thinking in an academically approved setting will have a liberating effect on minds that have been conditioned to conform to traditional education. Confidence in the expression of one's own ideas is further fortified when the creative thinking activities include a strong academic base. The discipline of creative studies has accumulated fifty years of history, literature, research, reports, and resources for the understanding and teaching of the academic discipline of creativity, which includes the creative person, the creative process, the creative product, and the creative press (climate for the expression of ideas and opinions). When the academic discipline provides a foundation for experiential learning, the student learns not only the "what" of the application but also the "why" of the understanding.

The collection of creative thinking strategies practiced in a problem-solving class removes the old barriers to freedom of thought and establishes new habits of mind. The four recognized cognitive factors of creativity become a familiar standard. They are:

- Fluency of ideas (the capacity of the mind to produce quantities of ideas and alternatives by making mental connections, both obvious and obscure).
- Flexibility of thinking (a preparation and pattern of thought that relies on a broad base of knowledge and information rather than narrowly focusing on single categories; a flexible mind can see an issue from more than one perspective, and the resolution of differences and polarities depends upon mental flexibility for the cooperative solving of mutual problems).
- Originality of thought (the mental practice of "thinking outside the box" and making remote connections to create ideas that no one else has thought of).
- Elaboration (attention to details and expanded connections, especially in aptitudes for applying and actualizing the original idea).

The quality of thinking that develops in a problem-solving class is a mirror of the kind of thinking that business is calling for when corporations report the need for innovation, new products, new systems of organization, and new strategies for profit making.

Habits of thought that are familiar to the teaching and effective practice of creative thinking and problem solving include the practice of deferred judgment; attitudes of flexibility; the habit of incubation, which capitalizes on the subconscious level of thought; and vision, the art of "looking into the dark in order to see."

Anyone who has participated in a brainstorming session is familiar with the principle of deferred judgment. A well-disciplined brainstorming group will frown on any suggestion of a judgment against any of the spontaneous ideas offered for a problem solution. The purpose of brainstorming is to generate new, original, untried possibilities for solving a problem; therefore, the discipline of avoiding immediate negative reactions to unexpected "wild and crazy" ideas has to be practiced. After the session, all the collected ideas are judged, and "crazy ideas" are modified to become possible candidates for implementation. The practice of deferring judgment can apply socially and politically, in personal relationships, and most other circumstances. Rushing to judgment is a good way to create more conflict than compromise. It takes a lot of practice to avoid immediate reaction to a new idea. Even experienced brainstormers are often guilty of knee-jerk reactions when new ideas offend their personal belief system.

Flexibility of mind is a basic requirement in times of conflict, whether in a home, at a board meeting, or in international diplomatic circles. Polarized positions have to find some means of compromise that is acceptable to both sides of the argument. The only way to resolve the problem is for participants to call upon the flexibility factor of their thinking. There has to be a mental conditioning for the art of compromise if the world is ever to work out its differences and find a path to peace.

One of the most effective strategies for producing original ideas for problem solving is an understanding and respect for the natural human process of incubation. When deliberate efforts to think up new ideas aren't working, and the energy winds down, a common practice in problem solving is to turn the problem over to the subconscious mind and turn off the deliberate search. "Putting the problem on the back burner" is an old and familiar description for the process. When the preconscious mind is in a more relaxed state (just before sleep, hypnogogic, or just after waking, hypnopompic), it is not uncommon for sudden mental connections to occur unbidden and produce unexpectedly the "Aha!" of a new idea. Incubation is a valuable tool in the collection of strategies for ideation.

The mental ability of visualizing or being able to look ahead to possible consequences of one's actions is important to any problem solver, and is an essential practice in problem-solving methodologies. The natural inclination of the mind to produce images can be trained to make imaging available deliberately and to enhance the problem solver's qualities of the visionary who has a natural "access to his imageries, to think with, create with, and to be entertained by. When we have taught people generally how to enrich imagination to such an extent, it is difficult to believe that they will not use their imagination more, develop it, refine it, and so become more creative" (Houston 1992, p. 417). Sidney Parnes has become a leading authority on the strategy of visualizing in the process of creative problem solving (Parnes 1992).

Although the teaching of creative problem solving is constantly creating new options for strategies that stimulate creative and other quality thinking, the structure and sequence of the process was established from the beginning and remains very much the same. Five distinct, logical steps provide the framework to be followed once the problem situation has been identified. A general practice that applies to all five steps is the alternate use of divergent (creative) thinking and convergent (critical) thinking. Brainstorming activates the mentality of divergent thinking. Judging and evaluating ideas activates the mentality for convergent (critical) thinking. The mental discipline for effective problem solving requires that players exercise the art of separating their imaginative divergent thinking from their analytical convergent, judgmental thought process. It has been said that "trying to do both is like driving a car while stepping on the brake and the gas at the same time. You use a lot of gas, but go nowhere."

THE ORIGINAL OSBORN-PARNES FIVE-STEP CREATIVE PROBLEM SOLVING SYSTEM

1. Step I—Fact Finding: Become totally acquainted with the problem to be addressed by brainstorming through a checklist of Who, What, When, Where, Why, and How each is related to the problem. Make notes. Throughout the system, participants make good use of quantities of paper for note taking, for capturing ideas, for doodling, and for recording information.

2. Step II—Problem Defining: When data on the situation and all its ramifications and connections have been gathered, the problem statement is considered. Again, the process of brainstorming is used to review the facts and create a list of possible statements beginning with the line "In what ways might we (for example) help to influence changes in the educational system?" This step is critical. The problem is viewed from many different perspectives, and from the collected list of possible statements, the one that best describes the real problem is selected. That statement will become the brainstorming topic for Step III—Idea Finding.

3. Step III—Idea Finding: Whether an individual or a group exercise, follow the brainstorming rule of deferred judgment to generate

great quantities of different options for solving the problem. Make use of strategies for stretching the mind to produce imaginative, out-of-the-box possible solutions.

4. Step IV—Solution Finding: List the criteria that will measure and compare the generated ideas. A matrix can be used to score the comparative ranking to choose the best solution.

5. Step V—Acceptance Finding: Make a plan of action. Use the Who, What, When, Where, Why checklist to cover the array of possible resources for helping to implement the best solution. When the solution requires a long-term time period, plans can be made for working on a number of fronts.

This sketchy description of the steps for the application of the Osborn-Parnes Creative Problem Solving Process makes the assumption that, in conducting a session, the facilitator will exercise a rich personal background of knowledge and skills for keeping a balance between the serious and the playful uses of the creative mind that are so central to the success of creative problem solving.

An experience in disciplined creative problem solving has lasting and general effects in the thinking patterns of participants. It doesn't matter much whether the participants are young students, degree candidates, business people at all levels, or seniors. I have watched problem solvers from all perspectives grow more involved, more trusting, and optimistic, more thoughtful and self-confident as they realized the pleasure and satisfaction of thinking and being recognized for their ideas. In university classes, the playful thinking exercises often needed time and a good dose of backup theory to persuade students, well-practiced in more prescriptive learning, that the class on creative problem solving was legitimately academic. Not only was it legitimately academic, it was a school experience that gave them an appreciation for the gift of a creative mind and its value for all time.

There is an important observation to be made here. Most of the discussion of creative problem solving and creative studies seems to gravitate around the teaching or training of thinking. There is another angle on the reason for education to pay attention to creative talent in the classroom: The reason is the need to provide opportunities for highly creative students, anywhere in the school system, from kindergarten to graduate school, to be recognized and better understood. There is an extreme diversity in the level of creative-thinking talent and potential in students of all ages. A significant percentage of the population, old and young, carries a rich genetic accumulation of talent for creative thinking and expression. One of the most significant pieces of research by Torrance found that at about the fourth-grade level, the natural uninhibited tendency for children's freedom of expression suffers a serious loss. The study became known as "The Fourth Grade Slump Study" (Torrance 1967).

When the urge for self-expression is consistently blocked by educational and social systems, or when attempts at creative expression meet with criticism and disapproval from the powers that be, a highly creative spirit will often react or retreat from participating in class activities. If the frustration of being deprived of self-expression is extreme, behavior may become extremely antisocial. Authorities in studies of juvenile delinquency have advised us that, when we are deprived of the power of expression, we are inclined to express ourselves in a drive for power.

I had a unique opportunity to observe the creative-thinking talent of inmates in a state prison some years ago. As a member of the community faculty at Metropolitan State University in Minnesota, I was scheduled to teach a class to one inmate who had registered for a special degree program that was being offered at the prison and had opted to take my class in creative problem solving. I made a number of trips to Stillwater (Minnesota State Prison site) and discovered a highly motivated, extremely superior student with uncommon creative talent. His name was Ed Poindexter, and he was hoping for a retrial that would correct the verdict of his trial and grant him his freedom. It was a long wait. In the meantime, he designed and prepared materials, and taught classes in *EsteemQuest* for groups of black inmates. The class was based on his research within the prison population that had found a serious lack of self-esteem among the black inmates.

According to Poindexter,

I became increasingly aware of the disturbing trend of inmates returning to prison in record numbers after they had been out for less than a few months—in many cases, only weeks—so I set out to find out why. It didn't take long to learn that these men had a critically deficient self-concept, namely low self-esteem, low self-confidence, self-worth, self-love, and a poor self-image (Poindexter 2004, 3).

The insights and work of Poindexter within that community of black inmates could make a valuable contribution to efforts for culturally equal educational outcomes and social equality.

There is reason to believe that the educational problem of a disparity between average achievement scores of white students and black students may have some of its origin in the nature of schooling that neglects programs that identify creative talent and fails to provide for its appropriate expression in problem-solving and other creative-thinking activities. That belief is fortified by an additional experience at the same prison. In the course of my visits, I was invited to teach creative problem solving to a special group of inmates who had been participating in a self-improvement program based on the book *I'm OK, You're OK*. It was a racially mixed group that was extremely responsive to the thinking activities and the problem-solving process addressed in the course. When the series of class sessions ended, the prisoners gave me a card, original in design, with signatures and comments by the participants. On the front of the card was the line "Thanks for Opening Some New Doors."

Educators have not only an opportunity but an obligation to open the "doors of perception" for all students. Getting the right answer on a standardized test is only part of the job. The enduring purpose of education is to provide students with a perception of the outer reaches of their talents and possibilities and, ideally, to give them a reason to continue to learn and contribute to their society for all of their lives.

The creative problem-solving process has found its way into the entire spectrum of diverse populations, always with an enthusiastic response from participants. A promotion piece for the 2004 Creative Problem Solving Institute says it this way:

> For fifty years the Creative Education Foundation (CEF) has helped people from all walks of life and all nations use deliberate creativity to make positive changes. Whether you are an engineer, educator, CEO, government official, parent, accountant, artist or inventor, CEF can help you make a significant contribution to the world at large and the world around you.

There is growing awareness among teachers in every part of the world of the place of creative education in the curriculum. They believe in its importance even when they lack the training to deliver it. Howard Gardner's popularization of the theory of multiple intelligences (Gardner 1993, 1986) has helped to bring attention to the accumulation of fifty years of research and leadership that mandates the teaching of creative thinking and learning at every level of education. Teacher education programs need to place a higher priority on developing teachers with confidence in their own creative ability to guide and cultivate creative-thinking and problem-solving talents in their students.

In the business of education, government and the general public have historically expressed plenty of interest in matters of educational funding, of building maintenance, of population and graduation figures, and bond issues. There are other critical educational issues of importance to personal lives, to the nature of society, and to the effective functioning of a democracy. We have been reminded that "America should sit up and take notice when the commission investigating the 9/11 terrorist attacks identifies failure of imagination as a key finding" and that "America's moral leadership in the world hinges on the engine of imagination, which it fuels with the values of freedom, respect for individual creativity, technology leadership, and innovation in thought and deed" (Sachdev 2004, 1). The judgments and initiatives of concerned and informed citizens are a valuable contribution to the business of designing the best possible education for our evolving national and international futures.

7

CREATIVITY = CAPITAL

We are facing a future where we will see changes all the time. How do we organize our corporations to face change? How do we get that through to people? It's not just a communications exercise, it's a mindset, it's a different way of thinking.

—Peter Russell

The first time I saw a bold public statement declaring that "Creativity = Capital" was at an art exhibition of the Joseph Beuys Multiples at the Walker Art Center in Minneapolis in 1999. The artist was Joseph Beuys, a native of Germany.

As someone whose professional life was dominated by the campaign to bring the academic discipline of creativity into practical application in both business and education, I felt the prominent display of a motto linking business and profit-making to creativity was a breakthrough of major personal significance. In my academic world, the translation of the elusive quality of creativity to the realistic dollars-and-cents profit side of the ledger was critical and long overdue. A year earlier, I had authored a book, *The Creativity Force in Education, Business and Beyond: An Urgent Message* (Bleedorn 1998). The Beuys authoritative statement was like an endorsement.

The exhibit was a manifestation of the artist's belief that we "should not see creativity as the special realm of artists, but that everyone should apply creativity to their own realm of specialization, whether it be law, agriculture, physics, education, homemaking, or the fine arts" (Beuys 1998). The literature accompanying the exhibit made it clear that he was talking about the basic issue of potential, the possibility that everybody has to do his own kind of art in his own work for the new kind of society. He was claiming that creativity is national income and that the human resource of creativity is the "new currency for the transformation of society." For some, the Beuys pronouncement may be a surprising claim. It is for everyone a reminder of a powerful reality: The capacity of the human mind for creativity and innovation is unlimited. Harvesting the creativity in a business translates to money in the bank.

That is exactly what educators of creative studies and proponents of creative problem solving have been telling students and the marketplace for fifty years, ever since the introduction of the concept of creative divergent thinking was identified as a specific intellectual process at a meeting of the American Psychological Association. The discipline of creative studies has its academic base in departments of educational psychology and studies of human behavior. The following observations are descriptive of the basics of creative education.

- Everyone is creative. It is part of the gift of being human. The creative process can be applied to any specialization, especially business. It is a force that needs to be set free. Philosophically speaking, "We have to realize that a creative being lives within ourselves, whether we like it or not, and that we must get out of its way, for it will give us no peace until we do" (Richards 1964).
- Creative expression is the basis of individual identity and, ultimately, of a positive self-concept. The natural inclination for creative thinking and behavior is traditionally discouraged in large, strictly organized institutions. It should be considered a human right to think and be heard in every organizational structure.
- Colleges and universities are offering creativity courses in increasing numbers throughout academic disciplines. The Creative Education Foundation in Buffalo, New York, has been the international center for research, resources, networking, and leadership in creativity for

fifty years. In addition to educational programs, centers for creativity and innovation throughout the world are serving the interests of business and other concerned communities.

- The discipline of creative studies includes literature, research, and resources on
  - The Creative Person (everyone)
  - The Creative Process (new, original ideas and their implementation)
  - The Creative Product (primary breakthroughs and secondary changes)
  - The Creative Press (climate/environment that encourages and rewards creative ideas and initiatives)
- There is a serious need to overcome the traditional polarities suggesting that the business community is focused only on the "bottom line" and that the educational community is too "theoretical and ivy-towered" to be of practical value. They need each other for the best work in the development of human and financial capital.
- Creative thinking can be taught if learners can practice the art of being serious and playful at the same time. Teaching creative thinking is largely a matter of establishing a climate of trust and freedom for the expression of new ideas and their implementation. Modeling an understanding of creativity and its value by upper management and CEOs in any business setting is critical to a climate for creativity and innovation throughout the workplace.
- A business that fails to exploit its creative intellectual human capital is suffering a serious loss. Its value goes way beyond the familiar emphasis on creativity as the "ultimate competitive weapon" to the perception of the creativity force as a critical ingredient in the achievement of a profitable, dynamic, enduring operation that works together in trust and respect for differences.
- The claim that "Creativity = Capital" is not a facetious one. An ideal workplace is one that believes in the claim, one that is inclusive rather than exclusive in its leadership, where every person has a sense of his significance and the opportunity to contribute to the shared goals of the institution, where efforts to create a modern self-organizing system depend upon the creative-thinking skills and

spirit of every player, and where meeting the challenges of a changing, competitive, dynamic global society invites and stimulates the
highest possible qualities of thinking, mutuality, and vision.

The beginning of the twenty-first century heralded an even stronger
appeal for new ways of thinking in the marketplace. In the year 2000, a
book appeared with the title *The Cultural Creatives: How 50 Million
People Are Changing the World* (Ray and Anderson 2000). The authors'
description of "Cultural Creatives" includes value systems that are not
readily quantifiable (like numbers on a balance sheet), but are qualitative assets that have a lot to do with driving the measurable profit line—
qualities like the following, excerpted from Ray and Anderson:

Authenticity: Your actions are consistent with what you believe and say.

Engaged Action and Whole Process Learning: You value personal involvement in the whole process of a project. You have a perception of the operation of the whole organization or system and your individual place
within those changing dynamics.

Idealism and Activism: You are motivated by work that makes a contribution to the organization and to society.

Globalism and Ecology: You can synthesize the fragmented pieces of information into an integrated system; you have concern for ecology and a
new way of life sustainable over the long run.

The Importance of Women: Whether male or female, you see women's
ways of knowing as valid—feeling empathy and sympathy for others, taking the viewpoint of one who speaks; being distressed about violence and
abuse.

Altruism, Self-Actualization, and Spirituality: You have a well-developed
social conscience, a sturdy but guarded optimism about the future, and a
concern about both social justice and the development of an inner life.
(2000, 8–15)

Fifty million Cultural Creatives with a mind and spirit for such value
systems could be a powerful force for change in any society. They are a
scattered force throughout the grand collection of organizations, social
institutions of all kinds, neighborhoods, and diverse communities. They
need to find each other. It is not that easy. Studies have shown that many

aspects of community life have been in decline since the middle of the twentieth century (Putnam 2000). People have an inclination to participate in community organizations of all kinds—churches, neighborhood organizations, political parties, and recreational leagues. The business community, with a belief in the profit-centered potential of the Cultural Creatives, can be a rallying place for the understanding and application of their qualitative values in service to company profit and growth.

At the same time, business leadership can take part in the public promotion of official academic initiatives that bring the discipline of creative studies into focus for business majors as well as for every student who is creating an educational background that will translate into an effective future career for a new kind of society.

A report of efforts by business leaders to influence education appeared in an article by William Coplin (2004). Under the title, "Businesses Need to Dive into Education," the author had a fundamental reminder for teachers: "Teachers consistently violate the Hebrew proverb, 'Do not confine your children to your own learning, for they were born in a different time.'"

The business community, from large corporations all the way down to start-up entrepreneurial operations, has good reason to be supportive of educational programs that offer classes in the specific study of creativity and innovation. It is appropriate here to make an observation about the understanding of the word *creativity*. It is taking so long to correct the myth that creativity is synonymous only with the arts and freedom of expression. Actually, creativity represents a powerful force for complex, original thinking in any field of human endeavor. The working of the mind and the attitudes of spirit that create a new idea are the bedrock of the process of creativity. *Innovation* is said to be related to the implementation of the original idea. The act of creation has not taken place until both the new idea or problem solution has been originated and the implementation of the solution has been accomplished. Both terms together define the total concept of creativity.

It is significant that the current marketing of conferences and workshops on creativity and innovation for business is promoting sessions with titles more focused on the term *innovation* than on creativity, for example: "The People Side of Innovation," "Innovation: A Business Trend in the Making," "Process, Structure, Tools for Innovation," "Idea

Futures for Innovation," and so forth. Companies and individuals are spending substantial sums of money to learn after graduation what could have been learned in the process of acquiring academic degrees and certification. Background in the understanding and practice of creative, innovative thought and application belongs in the requirements of any business major; it shouldn't have to be delayed for on-the-job training. Academic records that predict a candidate's capacities for new ways of thinking and new initiatives on the job could go far in selecting effective, productive new appointees.

Traditional, bureaucratic practices in higher education need vigorous encouragement from the business community to integrate studies of quality thinking, human potential, and human behavior with the existing requirements often focused on data collecting and analysis, counting and measuring, venture capital, and so on. Business funding for training and development programs in creativity and innovation could become redundant and could be channeled to other purposes if the workforce graduated with knowledge and experience in creativity, innovation, and problem solving.

Another major message for the marketplace was added in 2002, with the appearance of Richard Florida's book *The Rise of the Creative Class*. The message is loud and clear. The importance of creativity to our economy is real and growing.

Traditional systems of organizations, based on vertical command-and-control bureaucracies, were designed to discourage creativity in every section of their operation—the shop, the boardroom, new products, sales, accounting, research and development, human resources, public relations, and everywhere else. New ideas for change and innovation had little chance of being heard. The unlimited resource of the human mind for new ideas and their implementation has been squandered for many years.

Reports of business students in masters in business communication (MBA) classes on creativity in the 1990s were consistent: The major problem or challenge in the corporation was the difficulty of upward communication. The frustration level of creative members of the workforce over the rigidity of the system was causing a sizable economic loss. MBA graduates in positions of authority were so limited to quantitative factors that the important revenue-producing value of qualitative factors, like new ideas, initiative, vision, and systemic thinking, were ignored, silenced, or lost forever.

As an educator engaged with groups from the business community in the late 1990s, I was dismayed to learn of the disdain that some business leaders expressed for the educational system. I was advised to take the term *educator* off my business card because education was considered by practical, down-to-earth business people to be just so much academic theory with no practical value, and my identity as an educator would discourage their interest, even though I was teaching in university entrepreneurship and graduate business programs at the time.

Attitudes of that kind could easily be left over from the past, when plant owners began to hire college-educated engineers and MBAs to oversee the factory operations. With considerable book knowledge, but little experience in the actual workings of the factory—without the intelligence of the men who ran the machines—these new recruits would propose complicated systems and ideas that inevitably failed, and at worst, brought production to a grinding halt (Florida 2002, 65–66). Business could create a win-win system if they could influence education to design learning that would have the benefit of teachers who were, in the terms of Harlan Cleveland, "practical academics and reflective practitioners."

Talents for creativity and innovation function best when the work environment is compatible with the creative process. There would be small gain if universities prepared graduates of MBA programs with all the creative and innovative thinking skills while the business culture was busy maintaining the old practices of prescriptive management and control. Organizations can learn to foster a creative environment and to trust workers to be competent and responsible. A culture that encourages growth and positive change is based on a philosophy that "encourages ambiguity and risk-taking; accepts, encourages, and learns from mistakes; promotes an entrepreneurial atmosphere; displays a positive attitude toward change, and a positive orientation towards learning; and encourages appropriate humor and a sense of playfulness" (Miller 2001).

Whether in the laboratory or the library, creative thinkers want to be left alone and enjoy the freedom to think. What creative workers value in common is to be part of an organization that gives them the freedom to be creative, that values their contributions, that provides challenging work projects, and that has procedures for providing resources around new ideas. Companies that offer such an environment will be likely to attract and hold on to creative talent that can be expected to have a positive impact on the bottom line.

Schools and universities that respond to the changing nature of the workplace by requiring courses in creativity and other higher-order thinking processes free the mind and spirit of the learner. They not only serve the students' academic development, but also provide effective candidates for new kinds of positions in new kinds of businesses.

A learning organization understands that the success of the business is determined to a considerable degree by the product of its employees' thoughts and interactions—how they listen, communicate, dialogue, and relate to each other and to the customers. Most management is ultimately all about people. Being part of an effective work group requires not only complex thinking on the part of the individual but also the capacity for interdependence on the part of the team members. Steve Grossman (1988) was among the first to identify the "Four Faces of Creativity" that contribute to the success of a work team. He argued that all humans have some form of creativity and that the combination and complex interdependence of everyone's specialization makes the difference in the successful outcome of the team project. Here is a brief description of the four special creative styles (Grossman 1988):

> *The Creative Analyzer*: Interest in facts; agility with data and figures; attention to detail; pursuit of the total picture and its logical connections.
>
> *The Creative Imaginator*: Strong preference for imaginative thinking; speculates on possibilities; perceives relationships; appetite for change and risk-taking.
>
> *The Creative Implementor*: Highly organized; energetic; task oriented; juggles the details and keeps the system moving and on time.
>
> *The Creative Collaborator*: Good listener, good laugher; talent for bringing harmony to diversities; empathic; friendly and trustworthy. (7–8)

It may come as a surprise to see analysts identified as creative. I can assure you that it is a perfectly reasonable claim. During the 1980s, when I was presenting seminars and workshops on creative thinking for Internal Auditors International conferences, I learned to expect a substantial number of participants to have superior talents for creative thinking, analysis, and problem solving. The best auditors are not merely "number crunchers." They add talents for perceptive, imaginative, systemic thinking. They may even rely on a gift of intuitive insights. The common habit of making assumptions about a complex person on the basis of a single, simple categorical label distorts understanding of the human system and squanders the unlimited possibilities of the human intellect to serve the organization.

Every function of society, including government, is faced with the challenge of perceiving the reality of the connectedness of interactive systems. Honest communication and perceptive, open minds at the negotiation table are prerequisite to sound judgments. Schools have an obligation to teach and model the practical use of the unlimited resources of the human mind in the business world and everywhere else. Designated educational leaders need lots of help from the undesignated leaders in society to make the structural and content changes in the educational system at every level. One of those fundamental changes is official action that would add the specific teaching and practice of quality thinking to curriculum requirements.

Because of the expanding use of groups and teams in organizations, it is increasingly important that all involved players have acquaintance with some of the many studies that identify personal strengths and individual aptitudes like the Myers-Briggs Learning and Thinking Style Inventories (Myers 1980) and the Personal Profile System (Schmidt 1994). Successful groups are those that can forge a collection of individual specializations and styles into an interdependent, compatible task-performing group. Any member of a workforce whose educational record includes serious studies of human behavior, individually and as a member of a group, is better equipped for effective group performance.

The research and writing of the late E. Paul Torrance, leading scholar and international authority on creative education, has always had application to the world of business. The Torrance Tests of Creative Thinking (1980) were developed in the mid-1960s, and have been identifying and predicting creative talent in children and adults all over the world for almost fifty years. Attempts have been made to promote the use of the tests in business organizations looking for an indicator of creative talent in job applicants and in assigning members to task-performing groups. The current interest in *The Rise of the Creative Class* (Florida 2002) may serve to open the doors for the use of Torrance Tests of Creative Thinking in progressive business settings.

The last major contribution of Torrance for the public understanding and identification of superior creative persons was his development of the concept of Beyonders. He defined Beyonders as those persons who do their very best, who go beyond where they have been before, and who go beyond where others have gone. His research led to the design of an instrument that differentiates the behavior of Beyonders from that of their contemporaries (see chapter 5 for a list of the common characteristics of the Beyonders group; Millar 2004, v).

Isn't it significant that the qualities of Cultural Creatives have a strong resemblance to those of Beyonders? The explosion of attention to new insights into the human resource of the fully functioning mind is a constant reminder of the evidence that all of human affairs are genuinely and irrevocably connected. Society will be better off when it acts on that belief.

8

EDUCATING FOR LEADERSHIP

Therefore it is in the best interest of the species, from an evolutionary point of view, for individuals with problem-solving attributes, as
well as those possessing other creative and innovative traits, to be
recognized. This requires an attitude and a system directed to the selection of those who would also serve the species' interest and not
only the interest of the individual.

—Jonas Salk

Certainly the schools are in a preferred place for doing what Jonas Salk
was talking about. If society is going to have the benefit of leadership
with "creative and innovative traits," ready to "serve the species interest
and not only the interest of the individual," all of educational programming has to carry that deliberate purpose of the common good in its
design. There is evidence of growing public awareness of the kind of
enlightened leadership needed for the complexities of governing in an
integrative, diverse global community of nations.

There was a time in history when it made some sense for organizations
to be designed as closed systems, with well-established guidelines and policies spelled out in detail and firmly fixed, with the expectation of a long,
consistent organizational life. The accelerated rate of change in society and

the "global village" has changed all of that. An institution that adheres to yesterday's closed system of leadership built around traditional absolutes of inflexible hierarchical power and influence predicts its own ruin.

Closed systems breed attitudes of excessive caution and inflexibility; behaviors tend to be conformist and submissive; closed systems create a climate of conflict, competitiveness, and negativism; thinking habits reflect an either/or mentality rather than both/and mentality; and the work environment operates on protection of personal power and status.

Open systems, on the other hand, support attitudes of self-confidence and the capacity to entertain new ideas; behaviors trend toward initiative and innovation, trust, and cooperative teamwork. Participatory decision making and group problem solving characterize the organizational climate. The work environment is supportive of honesty, integrity, responsibility, and involvement.

Current trends in perceptions of leadership are looking for ways of decentralizing the process in the nature of open systems, while at the same time globalizing the vision. As an educator in the field of creative studies and a student of leadership and human behavior at United States International University in the early 1980s, I began to wonder about the relationship between the educational experience and the new understandings of effective leadership in the dynamically changing futuristic world that was coming to be (Burns 1978). During my readings in search of an inspiration for my doctoral study, I came upon a statement about creative leadership that gave me the idea for a dissertation. I would investigate the relationships between education and creative leadership for a global future. The statement I had found provided a specialized identification of qualities of creative leadership as the author had observed them. Many reflected the qualities of the creative person as I had learned them:

> An extraordinary capacity to grasp with great rapidity the unprecedented elements of new situations as they developed; an inner security; the freedom from self-absorption which enables a leader to keep his mind sensitively attuned to what is happening outside himself and to empathize with the feelings of those who make up the political community; relevant knowledge; excellent reasoning powers; and good intuitive judgment of people and situation. (Tucker 1977, 383–93)

Tucker's description of creative leadership from an article in *Political Science Quarterly* in 1977 might seem dated and irrelevant, if it weren't so valid in terms of much of the nature of leadership needed today in the first years of the new century. Time has passed since my study, but little has been done to acknowledge and address the need for new ways of teaching and thinking with creative leadership in mind. There has been an acceleration of courses in leadership in higher education business programs, but many academics have been better at teaching the theories and their research studies than at identifying and cultivating the complex and visionary thinking processes that underscore effective leadership. Having the necessary information is one thing. It is the effective processing of the information that serves the crucial business of wise decision making.

The plan I arrived at for my study was to compare the perceptions of three different samples of populations regarding the identification of talents critical to effective leadership in the advancing global age. Data were gathered from subjects representing educationists, college students, and business leadership. I started with the circulation of questionnaires handed personally to participants at a national conference of the Education Division of the World Future Society in Salt Lake City, Utah, in 1982, as they left the conference room following one of the major addresses. They were asked to list the qualities they perceived to be important for effective leadership in a global future. Their combined responses provided a list of thirty-three talents, arranged here in alphabetical order (Bleedorn 1988, 3):

1. Academic Skills
2. Action Orientation
3. Ambiguity (tolerance for)
4. Change Agent Qualities
5. Communication Skills
6. Commitment to Service
7. Cooperative (Attitude)
8. Curiosity
9. Creativity
10. Decision Making
11. Empathy
12. Energy and Health
13. Facilitating Skills

14. Flexibility
15. Futures Orientation
16. Goal Directed
17. Honesty
18. Humor (Sense of)
19. Humanistic
20. Identity and Self-Concept
21. Information Retrieval Ability
22. Listening Ability
23. Moral/Ethical
24. Multilingual
25. Other-Oriented
26. Organizational Ability
27. Pluralistic Attitudes
28. Problem-solving Skills
29. Risk Taking
30. Spiritual Awareness
31. Synthesizer
32. Visionary
33. World Focus

The two additional populations of college students and business leaders were added for the second round of the survey. Subjects were asked to:

1. Select and rank order from the list of thirty-three talents the five that they considered most critical for effective leadership in a global future.
2. Select and rank order from the list of thirty-three talents the five that they considered to be best addressed in current educational practices.

When the data were all analyzed, the basic results of the research in the combined group of subjects were as follows (Bleedorn 1988):

1. Out of talents perceived to be of primary importance for global, futuristic leadership, a majority were not perceived to be adequately addressed in current American educational practices.

2. Perceptions of all three surveyed groups reflected a need for the continuation of traditional learning. However, talents with particular relevance to the emerging role of leadership as described in the literature (Burns 1979)—that is, empathy, vision, tolerance for ambiguity, and humanistic attitudes—were rated low in priority by the three groups.

3. Based on the finding that the talent for creativity was ranked highest in leadership talent priority by the composite group, and that attention to this talent in educational practices was perceived to fall short of the mark in terms of its perceived importance, it was concluded that the development of creative potential has been a comparatively neglected talent in general educational practices.

Additional analyses were made and findings reported in the total study. Among the results was a list of talents significantly distinguished as being addressed by educational programming (alphabetically listed): academic skills, communication skills, goal-directed attitudes, information-retrieval skills, and organizational ability.

Talents significantly distinguished as not being addressed by educational programming (alphabetically listed): ambiguity (tolerance for), commitment to service, curiosity, empathy, humanistic attitudes, moral/ethical values, multilingual skills, other-directed attitudes, spiritual awareness, synthesizing (systems) mentality, visionary thinking, and world focus.

Publication of the book that reported the research, *Creative Leadership for a Global Future: Studies and Speculations* (Bleedorn 1988), created some interest among scholars and academicians, but little evidence of interest among educational practitioners or the general public. It would be interesting to repeat the study now, some twenty years later, to see if the comparison between global leadership qualities and educational programs would show a greater degree of integration. Certainly the current state of world affairs is placing a greater urgency on education for effective leadership nationally and internationally in the hope for world peace.

Most serious students of leadership have become acquainted with the seminal work of James MacGregor Burns, who had a lot to say about the mutuality of leadership and followership observable in systems responsive to our changing social and economic patterns. He suggested that effective leadership is "no mere game among elitists and no mere populist response, but a structure of action that engages persons to varying degrees throughout the levels and interstices of society so that only the inert, the alienated and the powerless are unengaged" (Burns 1978, 3). Since education is everybody's business, the time has come to engage the public in the mutuality of leadership and followership necessary for the development of educational experiences with effective leadership for a global future in mind.

Harlan Cleveland, eminent political scientist, public executive, and founding dean of the University of Minnesota's Hubert H. Humphrey Institute of Public Affairs, has been for years and continues to be a powerful spokesman for the obligation of society and its educational systems to produce international leadership (Cleveland 1993). He made an explicit challenge to educators in an article for *Twin Cities Magazine*: "This information to understand our tools and our purposes, and especially to relate them to each other, is not carried in our genes. It has to be learned. So we educators cannot cop out; equipping minds for leadership ought to be what's 'higher about higher education'" (Cleveland 1980, 27–28).

Studies of leadership include a distinction between "designated" and "undesignated" leadership. Designated leaders would be those who are officially recognized and titled leaders. We depend upon them to provide guidance and resources that support what needs to be done to move the institution and society into new and improved directions. They are publicly empowered and rewarded for their responsibilities of meeting the challenges of change and creating new directions that serve the growth and objectives of the institution.

There are also the undesignated leaders who have no official title but who see the current and future needs of the institution and are motivated to offer themselves as catalysts to help make changes. They are often those who have no great interest in public positions of power and influence but who have the necessary knowledge, insight, and vision, accompanied by the energy and spirit for contributing to a cause. Undesignated leaders are not intimidated and silenced by traditional formalities. Their urge to make a difference in society and its institutions can be a powerful force for change.

If we are looking for leadership that would serve the species' interest and not solely the interest of the individual, attention will have to be paid during the years of mandated formal education to cultivate thinking attitudes that open the doors of perception to the entire interrelated diverse factors of society. Leadership talents like empathy, humanistic attitudes, multilingual capacities, vision, world focus, and a tolerance for ambiguity that were perceived to be neglected twenty years ago may be given more educational attention now. Maybe not. It would be extremely interesting to know what has happened educationally in the meantime.

Actually, we don't have to wait for the results of research studies to know that even advanced degrees from prestigious universities are no guarantee of effective leadership that serves the species' interest. Standardized tests can measure some kinds of learning. Reading and math skills are of fundamental importance. But the complex thinking required to process the ever-increasing flow of information in ways that plan ahead and make wise judgments—that kind of complex thinking demands specific educational attention to the intellectual development of future leadership.

The pioneer work on leadership by Burns (1978) gave us specific descriptions of two distinctly different types of leadership: the transactional and the transforming. He says that the relations of most leaders and followers are transactional—leaders approach followers with an eye to exchanging one thing for another. The organizational structure is based on a hierarchical chain of command that determines, to a large extent, the directions for any growth or change. Communication is essentially downward. Upward communication has little chance of being heard. Tradition and status quo define the general approach to transactional leadership—the exchange of one thing for another.

Transforming leadership, on the other hand, is more complex. It is also more potent. The transforming leader "looks for potential motives in followers, seeks to satisfy higher needs, and engages the full person of the follower. The result of transforming leadership is a relationship of mutual stimulation and elevation that converts followers into leaders and may convert leaders into moral agents" (Burns 1978, 4). In some instances, transactional leadership has been equated with the old style of "management" and transforming leadership equated with the new style of genuine "leadership."

The business community has seemed to be more aware of the need for change in organizational leadership than the institution of education. Their literature, conferences, and public media reports have been making more references to the need for organizational change than the public literature of academia. Peter Russell (1992) was among the early proponents for change with his book *The Creative Manager: Finding Inner Vision and Wisdom in Uncertain Times.*

Another early publication, *Creative Work: The Constructive Role of Business in a Transforming Society* (Harman and Hormann 1990) spoke of the awareness and cultivation of personal empowerment and the discovery of "one's own deep wisdom and understanding of the truth of the times." They believed that business had become the predominant institution in modern society and would have a strong hand in reshaping the future.

As an educator, I want to protest. Didn't we believe in the beginning that an educated electorate was critical to a democracy? Didn't we always depend upon education to deliver the learning and the attitudes that preserved and strengthened that democracy? My entire teaching career had an underlying philosophy and belief that I was helping in a small way to preserve American values and to shape the future of the country and the world by instilling in students a belief in themselves and in their capacity to contribute to their society. A patriotic fervor had always had a defining place in my personal teaching formula. I don't think that is unusual among dedicated teachers. I may be ready to acknowledge some failure on the part of institutionalized education to create a voting population of quality thinkers, but I continue to believe that a concerned public can influence the system to redesign itself as a force for positive change from transactional leadership or management to a more realistic and inclusive transformational model of a new kind of leadership for a new kind of world.

It seems that the institution of business has been more visible than the institution of education for evidence of change agentry. The threatening times in our country and in the world can't wait much longer for a new system of educational leadership that capitalizes on the knowledge and spirit of everyone involved in the business of education. The need is for the activation of educational entrepreneurs who will work to create programs that serve the development and potential of all children and youth. It is imperative that the concerned public work with educators now for a reinterpretation of educational leadership that will be less stratified and "more egalitarian and dependent on individual responsibility, initiative and constant, open communication between individuals regardless of organizational rank. Direction and discipline will come from within, not from above, through interaction among colleagues at all levels" (Drucker 1989, 7).

There is a significant collection of educators within the system who are potential change agents and who have legitimate ideas for positive change in their profession. They are the educational intrapreneurs. Gifford Pinchot and Ron Pellman (1999) said of intrapreneurs:

> Because they closely resemble entrepreneurs, we call the people who turn ideas into realities inside an organization "intrapreneurs." The intrapreneur may or may not be the person who first comes up with an idea. Intrapreneurs roll up their sleeves and get things done. They recruit others to help whether working on an idea that was originally their own or building on someone else's. (16)

Pinchot and Pellman (1999) provided a detailed description of the concept of intrapreneuring as it relates to innovation in the business world. The same five components of innovation can apply also to innovation in education. They are the crucial roles of idea people, climate makers, intrapreneurs, sponsors, and the intrapreneurial team. Included in their book are specific recommendations for senior leadership and middle managers who recognize the need for change and innovation in their system.

Change agents anywhere are usually characterized by their creative spirit, their vision, their motivation to make something better, their tolerance for ambiguity, and their inclination for risk taking. They don't do foolish things to annoy the hierarchy or risk being fired, but manage to maintain the courage needed to be an innovator. Having some acquaintance with the inside workings of an educational bureaucracy, I am aware of the risks of change agentry when the organization is governed by a traditional bureaucratic power system. I am also aware of the possibilities for educational change when designated leadership listens and collaborates with undesignated leadership to implement new ideas that contribute academically and productively to the institution.

Things take time. Harlan Cleveland (1984, 2) once described leaders as the "first birds off the telephone wire." It is an interesting analogy. We have all seen a long line of birds perched quietly on a telephone wire and watched when suddenly, at some mysterious moment, one of the birds takes off and has a guaranteed, immediate following of all the rest of the flock. In human affairs—whether in business, education, society, or anywhere that people gather to work together for a cause—some urge or instinct can move a leader to initiate change and make a difference. Cleveland believes that most of the real leadership in promoting change comes from citizen activists who are not preoccupied with power or personal publicity. They are people "whose concern exceeded even their confusion."

Maybe business and education are not enough alike to make a legitimate case for educational entrepreneurship and intrapreneurship. But surely the human expectations of education for the intellectual, moral, and physical development of students are at least as important as the economic purposes of business. The deliberate teaching of higher-order thinking toward the goal of intellectual development would also serve the educational purpose of moral development. Isn't it reasonable to think that education could recover its place as the prime mover in the development of smart, visionary, moral, and responsible leaders of good will to which a true democracy is entitled?

9

THE EVOLUTION
OF A GLOBAL INTELLECT

Whether humanity is to continue and comprehensively prosper on Spaceship Earth depends entirely on the integrity of human individuals and not on political and economic systems.

—Buckminster Fuller

There are no passengers on Spaceship Earth. Everybody's Crew.

—Marshall McLuhan

It is not a simple matter to make a great leap forward to the perception of a new world order. Since the radical changes in science and technology that made everyone a global citizen, there has been a new demand on every citizen to change his or her habits of thinking. To maintain a harmony of differences in the world, everyone will have to shift to a higher level of thought that includes both world affairs and local traditions. Educational systems everywhere are beginning to realize their responsibility to provide learning experiences that prepare citizens for new international realities. Leadership, as well as every player in the drama of radical global change, will need to practice new ways of thinking.

In 1980, when I was shopping for a PhD program that reflected my educational interests, I found that United States International University (USIU) in San Diego offered an advanced degree in leadership and human behavior. Although the campus was more modest than impressive, the university's mission and its accreditation status fit my learning expectations. In addition, the fact that the student body represented a broad international sweep of countries and cultures was a certain match for my idealistic visions of "One World."

I graduated in 1985, with much more than an academic degree. The social encounters and learning experiences in the company of scholars from such a rich diversity of cultures was an incredible awakening to the process of the global transformation of human affairs and the role of education in its accomplishment. Because the study of leadership was prominent in my program, I began to wonder if the nature of our schooling would produce leadership equal to the complex demands of the emerging global, interconnected world and its future.

My dissertation was an effort to help provide an answer to that question. It was published by Peter Lang, New York, with the title *Creative Leadership for a Global Future: Studies and Speculations* (Bleedorn 1988). After seventeen years, the research findings and the message continue to apply; talents perceived to be of primary importance for global, futuristic leadership still do not seem to be adequately addressed in current American educational practices.

For better or worse, I took the vision of USIU seriously. In the words of its first president, William C. Rust,

> A University is primarily the gathering together of excellent teachers and qualified students in an atmosphere where they may interact with one another to develop understanding. It is a community where the learning process includes not only acquiring academic training, but also developing the skills of individual and group-living that are mandatory if the academic training is actually to be implemented. . . . The leadership which comes from a university like this is expected to have an impact on the local and worldwide community in the years that follow. Consequently, both students and faculty have a definite responsibility to make the most of the opportunities that the years at this institution provide. (Dil 2004, 41)

The years at USIU certainly fired me up to be an advocate for global education wherever possible for all time. As a student and scholar of creative studies, I found that its integration with studies of global education was a natural force for action. Adding the third factor, my history of membership and involvement with the World Future Society, has created a trilogy of purposes that has translated to a campaign for the deliberate teaching of creativity and other quality thinking processes at every level of learning in schools everywhere. It is a hard sell when centers of power in education are influenced by a status quo mentality. However, it is a logical direction for educational reform, and evidence grows that many professional educators and members of the general public have ideas and opinions of a like nature. They have only to find each other and together create a force for growth and change in what we teach and how we teach it in our schools and universities.

If, in the course of a student's formal education, specific requirements for studies of global education and international studies were assigned in every academic discipline and in every elementary and high school curriculum, society would not have so much trouble persuading the citizenry to appreciate and support the work of the United Nations. Their minds would be practiced in the art of seeing and thinking beyond national boundaries. The remembered words of a song sung to the familiar tune of "Finlandia" sends the message and evokes the emotion:

> My country's skies are bluer than the ocean
> And sunlight beams on clover leaf and pine.
> But other lands have sunlight, too, and clover,
> And skies are everywhere as blue and high as mine.
> O, hear my song, thou God of all creation,
> A song of hope for their land and for mine.

The signing of the United Nations Charter in San Francisco in 1945 was the best possible action for saving both Planet Earth and ourselves. Perceiving the world outside of one's immediate environment, and including the broad vision of an interdependent, diverse global family, does not come naturally to many minds. It requires a specific learning experience that changes old perceptions of nationalism without abandoning national identity. The new kind of world needs new perceptions based on knowledge of other lands, other cultures, and other values. Beyond the knowledge, it also needs direct encounters with people of the world, their differences, and our common humanity.

There was a time when university students spent vacation time hitch-hiking around Europe and other faraway places. Safer and cheaper travel abroad invited scores of young people to the adventure. The encounters and conversations with people of other cultures was a valuable base for the evolution of a global brain. Foreign travel for students now continues to be a privilege mostly for families with sufficient economic means. Exchange programs for foreign students serve very well to bring cultural differences and understanding into our consciousness. Progress in the direction of global awareness is being made in a random pattern, but many members of society have little appreciation of the radical changes in the world that have made global citizens of the general population.

For a long time, the term *globalization* seemed to be applied only to issues of global trade. The fact is that all people, all cultures, all societies, religions, languages, history, arts, and even humor, had almost overnight become an intertwined system, where all the differences were in a struggle to discover the most important thing about human diversities. We are discovering now that the most important thing about human differences is the enrichment they bring to the understanding of our common humanity and our common hope for a peaceful world for ourselves and for future generations.

Education has traditionally been designed for the "intellectual, physical, and moral development" of the individual. It was understood that getting an education would guarantee a higher level of social and economic standing in one's life. An appreciation for the freedom to live in a democracy added another expectation to the value of an education in many places. It became a commonplace reminder that citizens of a democracy were responsible for contributing to its proper functioning.

Education was expected to produce a population with an understanding of citizenship in a democracy, its accompanying privileges, and its responsibilities. Underscored was the responsibility to be informed regarding public issues and to vote. For a long time, public issues were confined to local and national matters. Then, suddenly, issues of national importance began to include questions with increasing international significance. Opinions that had required knowledge within the scope of national affairs now expanded to find a serious need for understanding of a more global dimension. The responsibility of citizens in a democracy remains the same—an understanding of the issues and a seriously considered vote; however, the responsibility has become much more complicated.

Independent learning and computerized information-retrieval systems will provide a certain level of preparation for the understanding of global issues for some of the population. However, there is no substitute for a vigorous academic effort to make global education a requirement everywhere in the world, especially where government grants citizens the right to vote. The evolution of the global brain depends upon educational leadership that not only teaches world geography and cultural differences but also places a high priority on the understanding of the critical need for a world population that sees beyond the apparent differences. Now the world has the need to perceive and acknowledge the deeper level of our relationships, which are defined by the ultimate fact of our common humanness. That kind of understanding can be taught and modeled in an enlightened education system by enlightened teaching.

Local, national, and international organizations working for global understanding, peace and justice, and intercultural understanding are moving societies in positive directions. Schools and universities have a responsibility to bring the message of global unity and understanding to the entire population during the mandated years of formal education and in every discipline of higher education. Efforts are being made within the educational community to internationalize American higher education. A 1998 publication on *Reforming the Higher Education Curriculum* (Mestenhauser and Ellingboe 1998) is an example of the integration of diverse academic disciplines around the issue of global education. The book is based on papers presented during a faculty/student seminar on the subject of internationalizing the curriculum. Titles include:

- Portraits of an International Curriculum
- Culture in Curriculum: Internationalizing Learning by Design
- The Role of Foreign Languages in the Internationalization of the Curriculum
- Internationalization through Networking and Curricular Infusion
- Mind Opening through Music: An Internationalized Music Curriculum

- Teaching about Cognition and Cognitive Development; How to Internationalize the Topic
- Global Academics as Strategic Self-Organizing "Think Tanks" (xi)

The list is encouraging evidence of a measure of action. However, the foreword of the book states that "The internationalization of American higher education is a major issue in higher education today. Yet, few would claim that our colleges and universities are very far along in providing an adequate international and intercultural background for all their students" (Mestenhauser and Ellingboe 1998).

If the educational system fails to move along energetically with all the changes in society and prepare the public mind for meaningful participation in current public affairs, it should come as no surprise that many political leaders will continue to exhibit so little understanding of the interdependent global realities. The dominant political practice is to treat problems of education almost entirely by the allocation of more funds, with little attention to the march of time and the accompanying need for major curricular and organizational change.

A more adequate preparation of the thinking level of the voting public and its leaders becomes more critical with time. Education is everybody's business. The bureaucratic stagnation of institutionalized education can be changed and programs updated by concerted citizen effort. Certainly, meetings regarding public issues of government, society, environment, peace and justice, international affairs, United Nations programs, and others should be making clear the integration between their cause and the education of the public mind. The practice of encouraging the attendance and involvement of serious students at public meetings is a strategy of enormous value in the beginning trend toward intergenerational thinking and problem solving. The old classification by age level, along with automatic assumptions made about the potential of youth to contribute, can be a genuine waste of human resources.

One of the most effective educational programs for creating world citizens is Global Classrooms: Model United Nations Curriculum, based on the kind of "learning by doing" that research has shown to be effective with students from elementary to upper-division college students. The experiential nature of Global Classroom learning enables students to gain new abilities in leadership development, conflict resolution, and problem solving. Objectives of the Model United Nations Curriculum are set forth in a document, *Creating World Citizens through Global Classroom: Model United Nations* (Lott and Schmitt 2004, 3–4).

Objectives of the Model UN are designed to help students to:

- become expert researchers as they investigate problems related to specific countries/interest groups and issues
- develop a personal view of and commitment to a positive future and an understanding of the changes needed to bring it about
- acquire skills of negotiation and consensus building as they role-play the representative of a particular country/interest group
- identify international, national, and local strategies for community development
- develop public-speaking and debating skills as they articulate "their" country's/interest group's stand on issues ranging from global warming to waste management
- engage in critical thinking as they are challenged to take into account the views and opinions of the many other governments and interest groups represented at the Model United Nations
- learn to respect and become sensitive to others as they interact with people who are different from themselves and their friends and neighbors (Lott and Schmidt 2004, 3–4).

Since funding for the United Nations Global Classroom Program is, in many cases, dependent upon grants from foundations, there is a limitation to the numbers of students who engage in the special program. The value of this experiential global learning experience for future citizens could justify its place in state educational requirements. Traditional official state requirements have been largely based on "know and understand, analyze, compare, investigate, explain, describe, and differentiate." A more complete listing of standards would include the learning process of "experiencing," in which learning becomes more real, relevant, and internalized. The Global Classroom experience of direct participation in a simulated meeting of the United Nations has a powerful effect on learning and global, futuristic thinking. Centers of power and influence in education have been slow in requiring creative, experiential learning and thinking because of the perceived difficulty of assessment.

The United Nations Association (UNA) provides another opportunity for students to explore world problems and develop a worldview. The National High School Essay Contest on the United Nations attracts the participation of serious high school students. The 2004 winner, Justin Krause from Steamboat Springs, Colorado, had the honor of speaking at the United Nations headquarters. His essay argued that, as the world becomes increasingly interdependent and humanity's greatest challenges extend beyond state boundaries, even national issues require international solutions.

Intercultural and international programs are attracting serious students from all over the world to U.S. universities. The presence and observations of these young people on college and university campuses are making a major contribution to the development of a global intellect in fellow students and in the community. Nadir Budhwani, a University of Minnesota student from Pakistan, observed in an article for a university publication,

> It would be great if the college and its alumni expanded their efforts to bring together people both within and outside of the college. It is high time that we, as torch-bearers of the College of Education and Human Development, educate others about the need to see that the diversity brought by international students is more of a strength than a risk/threat, thereby moving attitudes from ethnocentrism to global awareness. The world is very different now and continues to change. The outcomes of such changes remain as uncertain as changes themselves. However, one thing is certain: That we all have to take the responsibility to bridge the gap that exists between the U.S. American and international communities within the college. (Budhwani 2003, 21)

Somewhere along the line, before students reach the university level of education, there ought to be required learning experiences that would create a better understanding of the value of cultural diversities in the enrichment and evolution of human thought. The issue is too important to be left to chance. Public education is the assigned center of learning, not only of the past but also and most especially of the living present and possible future, where everyone "will be spending the rest of his/her life."

The dynamics of the times require more than textbooks, lectures, and assessment of learning. The most important global learning may require new, more flexible means of assessment. Understanding and empathy for cultures outside of one's own experience are not easily standardized. Most social studies textbooks provide only limited attention to United Nations concepts. Textbooks may be old long before they are worn out. Substituting the daily paper for the textbook helps teachers of excellence to update learning. They have the knowledge and skills to adapt official curriculum directives to teaching strategies more effective with the nature of their learners.

Effective teachers need the authority to improve on "the company line" when circumstances require change. Flexibility in teacher education programs should trump strict adherence to established curricula, and individuality in the selection of teacher candidates should cast a wide net. The nature of the times demands that official education grants new legitimacy to talents for creative teaching, a capacity for independent and complex thinking, and a mind open to new world realities.

Community organizations for peace in the world offer countless opportunities for involvement and leadership. Because of the natural integration between peace and global education, their mission deserves serious attention in classrooms everywhere.

Citizens, educators, parents, and students of all ages have an urgent need for intergenerational dialogue regarding the transition to a new kind of interrelated world where peace is possible through the activation of global systems thinking.

Global Education Associates (GEA), under the leadership of Patricia Mische, has been providing a global initiative for the advance of global understanding for many years. Her note as cofounder and president to the membership July 20, 2004, is a reminder of the mission and current state of the work of the organization. She writes,

Global Education Associates is one vehicle for raising voices of humanity and reason. For more than thirty years GEA has been a forum for multicultural dialogue on critical global issues. It is not enough to denounce injustice and war; it is also important to announce alternatives. That is why GEA has been at the forefront of creative thinking about alternative, nonmilitary paths to peace and security. GEA is committed to the development of global systems that can assure greater peace, human rights, democratic participation, and ecological balance not only for a few, but for all the world's people. Clearly, one voice is not enough. We need to speak in solidarity with one another. We need to speak effectively as well as collectively, in deed as well as with words. (Mische 2004)

Schools become more responsible to society when they join the public effort for global education as a basis for peace in the world. It is time for teachers, parents, students, peace advocates, and everyone else to be more active in providing information and feedback to educational power centers and political representatives. Likewise, it is time for educationists and legislators to listen and carry the information forward to leadership that ensures the globalization of education everywhere. A global intellect subtracts nothing from allegiance to one's own country. Complex thinking goes beyond the limitation of two-dimensional thought and integrates different perspectives into an enlightened system. The world is in dire need of new ways of thinking.

10

HOW GREEN WAS MY PLANET

We went to the moon as technicians; we returned as humanitarians.

—Edgar Mitchell

Before I flew, I was aware of how small and vulnerable our planet is, but only when I saw it from space in all its ineffable beauty and fragility did I realize that humankind's most urgent task is to cherish and preserve it for future generations.

—Sigmund Jahn, astronaut, German Democratic Republic

Of all of Earth's people, only a favored few astronauts have been privileged to see the Earth from space, hundreds of miles away. The effect on their consciousness is recorded in the personal statements of astronauts from all over the world. *The Home Planet*, a very large and heavy book, is an astonishing collection of color photographs of many different views of Earth from space (Kelley 1988). The photographs are enhanced by inspired observations from the space travelers.

Many earthlings have also arrived at a level of planetary consciousness and are exercising their sense of obligation for the protection of the home planet. The following statements by astronauts from many places are offered as a reflection of the depth of awareness and sentiment that is inspiring the intensity of leadership for environmental sustainability everywhere in the world.

The collection is introduced by astronaut Russell Schweickart.

We spend a great deal of time identifying and emphasizing the differences between things in our professional roles, including ourselves. And yet it is our common human experience, our shared fear, hope, joy, and love that link us as human beings beyond all differences. It is this shared personal impression of our home planet that has brought many of us together as the Association of Space Explorers. We hope you too will experience this new connection between us humans and our home planet as you read this book. It is the golden thread that connects us all and which I hope you will ponder long after the beauty of the specific images fades in your memory. It is what I ponder now and what I will marvel over the rest of my life. (Kelley 1988)

Astronaut Oleg Makarov added:

All the difference and difficulties can be overcome and the right words can be found when we are united by a common important goal—a goal that is really so simple—to make our conviction and knowledge more understandable to every dweller on Earth and to convey it to them more quickly. We hope that everyone will come to share our particular cosmic perception of the world and our desire to unite all the peoples of the Earth in the task of safeguarding our common and only fragile and beautiful home. (Kelley 1988)

The following quotations are representative of the collected impressions of members of the Association of Space Explorers in response to their experience in space (Kelley 1988):

In space one has the inescapable impression that here is a virgin area of the universe in which civilized man, for the first time, has the opportunity to learn and grow without the influence of ancient pressures. Like the mind of a child it is as yet untainted with acquired fears, hate, greed, or prejudice.

—John Glenn Jr., USA (136)

Instead of an intellectual search there was suddenly a very deep gut feeling that something was different—that it was beyond man's rational ability to understand, that suddenly there was a nonrational way of understanding that had been beyond my previous experience. There seems to be more to the universe than random, chaotic, purposeless movement of a collection of molecular particles.

—Edgar Mitchell, USA (138)

I would look at the Earth as it would be gliding underneath me and think, how everlasting all this is. After I am gone, and my children and my grandchildren, our Earth will still be gliding through the eternity of space in its measured, unhurried way.

—Vladimir Solovyov, former USSR (133)

During the light days I spent in space I realized that man needs height primarily to better know our long-suffering Earth, to see what cannot be seen close up. Not just to love her beauty, but also to ensure that we do not bring even the slightest harm to the natural world.

—Pham Tuan, Vietnam (85)

The first day or so we all pointed to our countries. The third or fourth day we were pointing to our continents. By the fifth day we were aware of only one Earth.

—Sultan Bin Salman al-Saud, Saudi Arabia (81)

It isn't important in which sea or lake you observe a slick of pollution or in the forests of which country a fire breaks out or on which continent a hurricane arises. You are standing guard over the whole of our Earth.

—Yuri Artyukhin, former USSR (71)

All of the astronauts' expanded perceptions of Earth—its beauty, its vulnerability, our shared human responsibility for its protection, the vision of its enduring presence—are evidence of a philosophical level of consciousness that happened in an experience of direct encounter. The scientific knowledge and preparation for the flight gave way to a breakthrough that added humanity and a sense of sacredness for the universe.

Breakthroughs in understanding happen all the time in the learning process. It is predictable that a real leap in learning is more likely to happen when there is a direct, purposeful experience. Serious educators are beginning to urge for more teaching that builds on experiential learning and engages the senses in an introduction to the abstract level of learning. Studies of the environment are especially suited to and often dependent upon a well-planned, purposeful field trip into the natural environment or a family outing that puts the learner into a direct sensory encounter with the real world of nature. Life in a small town or rural area provides a constant environmental learning experience for the inquiring mind. Teachers and parents can testify to the excitement expressed by students when they discover and learn about nature and the diversities of life in the field or stream or forest.

There is no more graphic opportunity for thinking of the interrelatedness of systems than the environmental studies of climate, earth, sea, air, and all the rest of the phenomena of nature. Opportunities for exercising the advanced thinking process of visualization are built into environmental studies when predictions of observable trends in nature are the subject of study. One of the arguments for the deliberate teaching of creativity and other quality thinking processes (Bleedorn 2003) is a promotion for capitalizing on environmental studies and futures studies content as vehicles for exercising the mentality of complex thinking. If official educational requirements for environmental education are not included in mandated state curricula at every level of learning, everybody loses. If recommended textbooks fail to address the issues of environmental protection, the Earth's future and the quality of life for future generations are in serious jeopardy.

The image that children have of the future has a considerable influence on their attitudes and behaviors. The positive expectations they have of themselves and the world around them is a powerful factor in their learning and achievements. As early as 1987, a project built on envisioning the future was conducted with children and reported in *Save Tomorrow for the Children* (Torrance 1987). The project was an International Scenario Writing task conducted for the Fifth World Conference on Gifted and Talented Children. It called for participants to write a scenario that would predict a positive image of the students' future.

The writing of scenarios is a familiar strategy in the teaching of futures studies and the making of predictions, according to the methods of the World Future Society. Scenario writers try to imaginatively predict what is likely to happen if certain trends continue with no interference. Action may then be taken to avoid negative consequences predicted in the scenario. Directions to participants in the Scenario Writing

Contest included these guidelines: "Try to express your image of the future through a scenario of not over 1,500 words. Make yourself the hero/heroine of your story. The story you are to tell is about what you expect to accomplish by the year 2010 and how you solved the problems and challenges during those years" (Torrance 1987, 2).

Youths from age nine to eighteen participated in the contest. More than five thousand scenarios from around the world were submitted and reviewed. A number of them are included in the publication. Many scenarios are positive and filled with imaginative ideas. Many also reflect some students' serious concern for the future and possible atomic disasters.

Lyrics for a song were written by the authors to express the essence of the students' scenarios. Here are selected excerpts (Torrance 1987, 4):

> Save tomorrow for the children.
> Take good care of today;
> Leave this old world
> Just as you found it.
> We will make our own way.
> Just save tomorrow for the children.
>
> Will the crystal-clear raindrops
> Still fall from on high,
> Beckoning roses
> To reach for the sky?
> Will there still be a place
> Where the wild things go free?
> Please tend the garden for me.
>
> If today were tomorrow
> Then I know who I'll be;
> Finally someone
> Would listen to me.
> And they'd all see the truth
> When I sang out my song
> But this time, they'd all sing along.

It would be interesting at this later time in history to hear scenarios written by thoughtful students. It would be equally interesting to make specific use of the strategy of scenario writing as it applies to the natural world—to investigate environmental conditions as applied to global land use, fresh water, the oceans and atmosphere, endangered species, climate and global warming, the wild places, and more.

Children and youth are all much smarter than we think. They are smarter than the standardized test scores tell us. They have a longer tomorrow than adults, and most of them think about it more than we realize. Studies of the environment built on experiences in the natural world can provide content for the practice of basic skills—reading, math, scientific observation and research, original creative art works, self-expression, and more. Students at any age can have stimulating, intellectual learning experiences through well-planned environmental curricula.

Urban communities also provide a setting for experiential, hands-on environmental studies. An example of community support for environmental learning is a program based in St. Paul, Minnesota, titled Eco-Education. That nonprofit organization helps teachers to plan and produce learning experiences based on current urban environmental issues like mercury and lead in our environment, the issue of air quality in the city, land use and green space in the heart of downtown, soil erosion prevention, the invasive species buckthorn, and more. Eco-Education collaborates with the Urban Stewards program that "engages students in active citizenship by supporting them in choosing and taking action on environmental issues important to them and their communities." It is reasonable to assume that environmental education programs of a like nature are going on in other communities.

The long-term value to students involved in practical learning that integrates school with community and student life with scientific and social realities cannot be overestimated. Learning becomes real and curiosity leads to answers and understanding in a way not motivated by the prospect of standardized tests. Education that makes use of daily news reports of environmental issues constantly reinforces the urgent nature of environmental problems. It is everybody's business to pay attention to stories like the removal of restrictions on logging in national forests, climate change, and global warming that will "considerably affect our societies and environments for decades and centuries to come." We have been reminded many times that "there are no passengers on Spaceship Earth. Everybody is crew" (McLuhan).

School programs and activities in support of environmental sustainability can create intergenerational events that bring educators, parents, and students together in a shared purpose that serves the entire community and helps to save tomorrow for the children. Initiatives for projects can come from students, parents, PTA, or teachers and administrators. Harlan Cleveland (1980), authority on international government and leadership, reminds us that people who can really get things done, and who can think with quality about what to do and how to do it, are a rarity. He tells us that they are rare—not that they are nonexistent. He challenges everyone to participate fully in the changing global environment, and suggests that most change in society comes not from top designated leadership, but "bubbles up" from the bottom. It is everybody's business and opportunity to serve the fundamental human task of preserving the environment for future generations.

Students have a right to understand what is happening to the world that they are inheriting. They are entitled to the knowledge of the ecological facts gathered from literature on environmental sustainability that we are cutting trees faster than they can regenerate, overgrazing rangelands and converting them into deserts, overpumping aquifers, and draining rivers dry. On our cropland, soil erosion exceeds new soil formation, slowly depriving the soil of its inherent fertility. We are taking fish from the ocean faster than they can reproduce. We are releasing carbon dioxide (CO_2) into the atmosphere faster than nature can absorb it, creating a greenhouse effect. As atmospheric CO_2 levels rise, so does the Earth's temperature. Habitat destruction and climate change are destroying plant and animal species far faster than new species can evolve, launching the first mass extinction since the one that eradicated the dinosaurs 65 million years ago.

The urgency of the Earth's environmental trends challenges educational leadership to give a higher priority to environmental education at all levels. The work of interrupting the ongoing loss of natural resources needs the participation of everyone. Young people have the greatest stake in the future of the planet. If they can understand the present facts

and draw on their natural instinct for looking ahead, they will be motivated to join the forces already at work to correct the public practices
that are threatening to deplete the finite resources of our planetary
home. Supporting educators who are promoting environmental programming for students and helping to connect schools to community resources for studies of environmental protection are valuable contributions for concerned citizens whether or not there are school-age
children in the family.

Countless organizations in this country and around the world are
working to acquaint people with current conditions and opportunities
for public service in behalf of the future of life on planet Earth. The
Sierra Club is one of the national organizations with local chapters that
recruit volunteers for active leadership in the shared challenge of the
preservation of healthy communities. The scope of their influence is international. Since issues of climate, global warming, the deep sea bed,
and the atmosphere are shared across the entire globe, the only way to
solve the problems is by working together. There are no frames or
boundaries in the natural world. The astronauts' view of our planetary
home from space didn't include the lines of political boundaries. We are
all part of the same dynamic, interactive, precious system.

An important step was taken in 2000 to ensure the environmental collaboration of all nations when the Earth Charter Commission approved
a final version of the Earth Charter, a declaration of fundamental principles for building a just, sustainable, and peaceful global society in the
twenty-first century. It is an expression of the great hope that all people
can be inspired to feel a sense of global interdependence and a motivation to make themselves responsible for the "well-being of the human
family and the larger living world." The purpose of the Earth Charter is
set forth in the preamble:

> We stand at a critical moment in Earth's history, a time when humanity
> must choose its future. As the world becomes increasingly interdepend-
> ent and fragile, the future at once holds great peril and great promise. To
> move forward we must recognize that in the midst of a magnificent di-
> versity of cultures and life forms we are one human family and one Earth
> community with a common destiny. We must join together to bring forth
> a sustainable global society founded on respect for nature, universal

human rights, economic justice, and a culture of peace. Towards this end, it is imperative that we, the peoples of Earth, declare our responsibility to one another, to the greater community of life, and to future generations. (Earth Charter 2004)

The Earth Charter is an extremely far reaching, internationally comprehensive, and dynamic system for the global realities of environmental protection and sustainability. Having its origin in world meetings in Johannesburg and Rio de Janeiro gives true global dimension and authority to its purpose.

The mandate is undeniable. The future of the environment can be guaranteed only with the determined effort of all the players in the world drama, in every society, and there is no time to lose. It is a perfect project for the integration of schools and society, the community, and the education profession. It is a perfect project for learning about the real world and the interactive, systemic nature of all of life. With initiative and leadership on the part of everyone, students can learn to play an important part in protecting the future of their earthly home. It is a time for personal action and resolve. Margaret Mead said it well: "Never doubt that a small group of thoughtful, committed people can change the world. Indeed, it is the only thing that ever has."

⓫

BALANCING SCIENCE, TECHNOLOGY, AND THE HUMANITIES

> Many of the problems that mankind faces today are the conse-
> quences of a disjunction between man's nature, his environment,
> and the creations of scientific technology.
>
> —René Dubos

Someone once asked, "Does technology reduce our capacity to think?" We might extend the question to ask, "Does technology reduce our capacity to live?" An increasing number of opinions are beginning to shed some doubt on the wisdom of the existing imbalance between the values we place on science and technology and the values we place on the understanding of human behavior, our human diversities, our intellectual development, and our human destiny.

Right up front, I want to admit to my own imbalances of background in favor of the humanities over the sciences. From the beginning of my education, I learned to avoid, whenever possible, classes based on numbering and analytical processing, sequential thinking, and logic. They gave me no pleasure. Lectures and literature by brilliant general systems thinkers in the realms of nature and universal order (Jaccaci 2000) were beyond my understanding or even any genuine interest. On the other hand, the qualitative studies of human intellect and behavior, of human possibilities and potential, were full of fascination and discovery for me.

I have no problem acknowledging and marveling at the achievements of science and the service to the world of the technological break-throughs, but to assign them an absolute top priority in the design for a human lifetime discounts much of what I have learned and observed of human nature. The behavioral sciences, although still a "science," are a different discipline from that of the natural sciences. The humanistic branch of the behavioral sciences has always seemed to do a better job of including the uncountable factors of the intellect in the formula for understanding the subtleties of human behavior.

One of my most treasured books is an autographed copy of a book by René Dubos, *So Human an Animal* (1968). The author, a microbiologist and experimental pathologist, was a professor at Rockefeller University in New York City in 1968. His book was a 1969 Pulitzer Prize winner. I don't remember buying the book or meeting the author for an auto-graph. It must be that I found it at a used book sale some time after its publication. In addition to the autograph, the book has the further en-richment of countless hastily scribbled notes and spontaneous observa-tions by some other reader. What makes it significant in my life is the fact that it was written at about the time that I entered the University of Minnesota, as a very adult student, to complete a bachelor's degree. As a result of an educational psychology course in group dynamics with E. Paul Torrance, I became addicted to studies of human behavior, es-pecially in relation to creative education, within which discipline Tor-rance was an early established authority.

It was some time during my studies that I began to have the uneasy feeling that the quantitative, behavioristic approach to the behavioral sciences was outstripping the more qualitative, humanistic approach. At the same time, there was increasing evidence that science, technology, and mechanization were beginning to dominate the human scene and the expectations of the future of the workplace, industry, the environ-ment, and educational priorities. When the ideas of Dubos came into my thinking, it was like a personal connection to a powerful scientific support system for my humanistic perceptions. I learned that an inte-gration was possible between the popular polarization of the sciences and the humanities, that they were interdependent disciplines, and that the educational system placed a limitation on intellectual development when it failed to include studies of philosophy and other humanistic courses in requirements for certification in the sciences.

As early as 1968, Dubos was seeing the long-term, troubling results of the domination of science and technology to the human side of life. He said:

> So far, we have followed technologists wherever their techniques have taken them, on murderous highways or toward the moon, under the threat of nuclear bombs or of supersonic booms. But this does not mean that we shall continue forever on this mindless and suicidal course. At heart, we often wish we had the courage to drop out and recapture our real selves. The impulse to withdraw from a way of life we know to be inhuman is probably so widespread that it will become a dominant social force in the future. To long for a human situation not subservient to the technological order is not a regressive or escapist attitude but rather one that requires a progressive outlook and heroic efforts. (1968)

A few years later, E. F. Schumacher made farsighted predictions about the future of the racing technological trends in his book, *Small Is Beautiful: Economics as if People Mattered*:

> Suddenly, if not altogether surprisingly, the modern world, shaped by modern technology, finds itself involved in three crises simultaneously. First, human nature revolts against inhuman technological, organizational, and political patterns, which it experiences as suffocating and debilitating; second, the living environment which supports human life aches and groans and gives signs of partial breakdown; and, third, it is clear to anyone fully knowledgeable in the subject matter that the inroads being made into the world's non-renewable resources, particularly those of fossil fuels, are such that serious bottlenecks and virtual exhaustion loom ahead in the quite foreseeable future. (1973, 147)

Both of these prophets of technological futures—one a scientist, the other an economist—gave us the benefit of their intellect for balanced and integrative thinking. The public arena and the marketplace often pay very little attention to complex kinds of thinking in systems with a time reality in the future. The level of thought that dominates the public mind has severe limitations, especially when there is the prospect of a fortune to be made. Single-mindedness and self-serving values usually trump concern for the public good and the quality of life for future generations.

We can't say that we were not warned. An article by Alvin Pitcher in the Harvard Business Review was a reminder of "The Importance of Being Human" (1961).

> More than forty years ago, this prestigious business school was publishing the thinking of concerned professionals on the profound impact of technology on the way people live, on the limits of human toleration for the stress of constant change and activity, for the mobility and mechanization dictated by a technological society, for the flood of numbers and statistics and survey results and quantitative calculations that define reality, and the depersonalization that follows when a computer is consistently substituted for a personal encounter. Add to that the observation on our educational system where "quality is being extensively sacrificed to quantity." (Pitcher 1961, 48)

Three crises were identified by Schumacher in 1973: the debilitating effect of technological overload on human nature, threats to the environment, and depletion of finite resources. The crises have been intensifying since his warning almost forty years ago. Now there is more public awareness of the fact that man does not have an infinite capacity to adapt to changing environments and that it is a myth that he can be endlessly transformed by technology. The reality is that there are biological and psychological limits to man's adaptability, and these should determine the frontiers of technological change.

Most human problems include such a collection of social complexities that the precise planning and study of the orthodox methods of the natural sciences alone are inadequate for their solution. It is becoming increasingly clear that there is a genuine need for more attention to the interrelationship of studies of technological science and studies of the human experience. Anything less is a denial of the reality of the complex, systemic nature of all things. Many problems of human lives and natural resources are the result of neglecting the integration of the different forces operating in the modern world, rather than ignorance concerning the separate forces themselves.

The institution of education is a good place to begin to develop minds that are well practiced in the interplay of differing forces. The bureaucratic procedures of recent federal government requirements that focus learning on the results of standardized testing run a numbers game that denies the individualistic human side of the learning process. Teachers and administrators are forced to concentrate their efforts on the science of numbers only if they want to avoid the punitive action and public embarrassment of low-ranking scores in their school as the prime indicator of their success in the classroom. Most of the truly enduring human values like personal identity, integrity, morality, fairness, loyalty, independence of thought, teamwork, and other character-related qualities have to be sacrificed to the authority line of quantitative data.

This is no radical argument to do away with testing. It is an appeal for official educational attention to a mandated balance between the science of numbers and the equally realistic science of human behavior and intellectual development. All it takes is the aptitude for the exercise of a higher-order thinking process that perceives the relationships between opposites and avoids the mindless competitive polarization between them. There is little argument for the claim that educational standards transfer to society. Training minds to make all their judgments on the basis of data, surveys, mathematical calculations, and scientific habits of mind is observable in the operating systems of business and politics. Positions are established, alliances made, and single-minded objectives are often pursued with little sign of interplay between the polarities. The energies that could have been expended to find accommodation between the two positions are spent in the unproductive defense of a single and often simple-minded position. The stagnation of mental development could be avoided in the educational process through specific curricula that teaches course content by means of teaching strategies based on the understanding and practice of quality thinking processes (Bleedorn 2003).

There is an indisputable logic in the claim that thinking is an art well worth learning, for "every important thing we do is affected by our habits of mind." Twelve years of mandated education with an imbalance between the scientific learning methods of quantitative analysis and assessment and the qualitative learning and thinking methods of individual differences and self-expression—those years can have a lasting effect on habits of thinking. Neglect of the human side of the learning equation sacrifices the opportunity of education to cultivate independence of thought, a positive self-concept, problem-solving capabilities, and a mentality for teamwork and community service.

Many teachers and administrators of excellence manage to insert the humanities and their respect for student diversities into their educational practices along with attention to federal testing requirements. A remarkable example of a renowned scientist, thinker, and educator is the late Otto H. Schmitt, former head of the University of Minnesota Biophysics Department, researcher and inventor. Even with his distinguished scientific career, his most important contribution was the inspiration he provided to students, colleagues, and the public during his career. He is said to have had "refreshing ideas about being a teacher." He thought that he could best educate his students by learning from them, and that he should be able to "teach others in two years concepts that took him three years to learn." He made observations about professors who continued to teach the same thing in the same way for thirty years (Schmitt 2004).

The preoccupation of educational leadership with scientific thinking and research seems to have lost touch with the equally important humanistic and philosophical realities of our diverse lives. In 1948 Omar Bradley is reported to have remarked, upon seeing the capacity of our nation to wage war, that we had achieved brilliance without wisdom. Knowledge and technological advances are not enough for the solving of society's problems. Without wisdom, society's judgments are based on a "win-lose, right-wrong, vested-interest perspective toward a process of engaging multiple world views, each producing its own truths" (Hassel and Spangler 2004, A5).

The intellectual level of paradoxical thinking is a prerequisite for a society and world steeped in a diversity of cultures, religions, and ideologies if we ever hope to achieve a more sane and peaceful world. If complex thinking were taught, practiced, and modeled during the process of education everywhere, the people of the world would understand more and fight less.

An interesting reference to the accommodation of differences between Western economic values and Native American spiritual beliefs asks the questions: "Should wild rice be considered as a crop to be domesticated for the purposes of economic development or as a sacred gift from the Creator? Is the role of humankind to subjugate nature with dominion and control, or to more humbly live in harmony with 'all that is'"? There are serious questions to be considered: Is science our only source of genuine knowledge, or might indigenous knowledge offer valuable understandings? Can "scientific" knowledge rightly be considered objective, or does objectivity remain an aspiration beyond our reach? Does science produce reality itself, or merely a map of reality that we find useful (Hassel and Spangler 2004, A5)?

Tensions between differing cultural views in the world will need to invoke higher-order thought processes. They will require a capacity to treat the tensions from broader, more humanistic perspectives than the familiar system of "vested interests." They will require creative, innovative thinking and problem-solving talents at a level of paradox where opposites can be translated to a win-win solution through the power of thought. If schools are serious in their stated objective of serving society, they will require the teaching and exercise of thinking strategies like creative problem solving, conflict resolution, and all the other practices of good teaching that call upon students to stretch the "muscles of their minds."

In some cases, the dramatic advancements of technology have had a greater influence on society and education than the other way around. Of course, technology is providing advantages, but a growing number of educators are calling attention to the need for students' relief from the overstimulation of technological games and screen time of all kinds. The claim is made that "as the process of interacting with the world becomes more passive, children are robbed of the process of being an active agent in their own lives." The capacity to solve problems is said to be underdeveloped to the degree that the term *problem-solving deficit* has been coined to describe the growing dependence of children on the instant gratification of the computer response. The antidote for the growing number of overstimulated, hyperactive, computer-dependent children is said to be regularly scheduled, uninterrupted quiet time for thinking. An article in the *Boston Globe* (Meltz 2004, E8) attests to its importance if we "want to raise children who can think critically, who can solve problems of all kinds—and we do, that's our mission—they need the chance to think uninterrupted."

Teachers at every level of learning can give students an opportunity to puzzle over thinking assignments that have no right answer but make use of all their individual store of knowledge and invite a tolerance for ambiguity rather than an instant right answer in a programmed machine. Cultivating habits of thought that remind students of the power of their independent brain helps to underscore their sense of personal identity and significance.

Thinking doesn't always require class time. Thinking can happen at any time during the day, even when the mind is "at rest." The incubation process of problem solving when the brain suddenly produces a solution without deliberate thought is a well-practiced strategy. Children at any age can be asked to think about questions like "Which is stronger —love or hate?" or "How are your brain and a computer different? How are they alike?" Playing with the interpretation of paradoxical ideas can engage the mind in the pleasure of thinking, even when there are no right answers. Sharing their personal interpretation of paradoxical concepts like the following can stimulate the exchange of independent quality thinking for advanced thinkers: sensitive warfare, quantitative idealism, analytical togetherness, critically creative thinking, violent pacifism, or scientific humanism. Teachers can design paradoxical concepts related to material to be studied. Student intellect can thus be more excitingly engaged in independent and creative thinking about course content than when memorizing facts for a test. Teachers should be prepared for the freedom to exploit students' capacity for creative thinking.

Computer literacy is a good thing, but it would be well to balance it with an equal store of actual literacy that prepares the mind for deep and philosophical thinking. After all, advanced degrees conferred on students of science as PhDs give them the honored title of "doctors of philosophy."

The World Future Society has been making predictions about the future of science for many years. In 2004, Howard Didsbury, World Future Society editor, edited a publication *Thinking Creatively in Turbulent Times*. One of the articles has particular relevance to speculations about the future of science. In it, Joseph Coates offered his predictions on "Where Science Is Headed." Some examples:

1. A continuing blurring of the distinction between science and technology. Generally, science is called upon where the identifiable limitations of current technologies demand a fresh basic look to find radically new avenues of improvement.

2. The distinction between basic and applied science continues to blur. There is a crack in the academic monopoly on basic research because many of these basic research projects end up in the hands not of universities but of nonprofit and government laboratories and private contractors.

3. Interdisciplinarity is increasingly important in research while largely ignored by academics and their universities. Almost all of the new leading-edge fields in science—genetics, brain research, and nanotechnology, as well as materials science, robotics, and automation—require interdisciplinary research and development. The university is, by and large, not comfortable in accommodating this intrinsic demand of contemporary research. As a partial mechanism for dealing with the need for interdisciplinarity, they often set up "institutes," which are more often than not only loosely linked to the basic science departments' teaching and curricula.

4. Credentialing in science is rapidly changing, expanding, and diversifying. This is a challenge to the traditional certifying by the university and is a response to the university's indifference and sluggishness in responding to new needs.

5. Globalization of both basic and applied research is rapidly progressing. Globalization has been facilitated by the end of the Cold War, which generated a superabundance of cheap, highly skilled labor in the Iron Curtain countries, and by the more recent emergence of highly skilled labor in China, India, and to a lesser extent in other countries. The quality of that foreign talent is an attractive complement to the U.S. base, in being stronger in theory but perhaps marginal in goals and commitment to practical applications.

6. Outsourcing is increasingly commonplace. It is virtually universal in some sectors of research and development, production, test, and evaluation. The key advantage is that it allows one to draw upon best available talent, while the cost is often lower and the flexibility much higher than if the work were conducted internal to the organization.

7. English is now the universal language in science. Young scientists—those under forty—are fully literate in English. The

professional universality of English facilitates the globalization in outsourcing.

8. In the United States, basic and applied science is increasingly falling into the hands of foreign-born scientists, in training in American universities and among those already established in the field. The policy issue needing to be examined is whether the growing dependency on foreign-born talent is good for the future of the U.S. research and development establishment and for our general competitive position in the world. The question is asked: Should companies be allowed openly or by subterfuge to replace a citizen by a foreigner merely to enhance the corporation's bottom line?

9. Ecology is the logical scientific base for all environmentalism and for the environmental movement. Regrettably, progress is slow, underfunded, and without a sound theoretical base. . . . We still see a tremendous amount of gratuitous conflict and disagreement with regard to environmental management and the future.

10. The scientific knowledge held by the public is pitiably thin and unreliable. The most conservative inhabitants of Capitol Hill are ever ready to block educational, medical, or other information they find ideologically obscene and to punish the perpetrators by budgetary cuts of constrictive legislation. The president's education program promises "No Child Left Behind" but at least as far as science goes, it is a joke. (Coates 2004, 16–22)

There are other predictions more related to specific branches of science. Those listed are the ones that have the most relationship to the issue of the integration of education with society. As a nonscientist, I am happy to leave that branch of learning to the specialists. However, there is a mutual challenge to both education and the natural sciences to find a way for their integration. There is plenty of evidence in the predictions for the claim that our education system has been lax in the preparation of its graduates for the effective interdisciplinary thinking so critical for the systemic realities. Science and the humanities have a need to respect each other and to value alternate disciplines in the opening of their integrative "doors of perception" that can move toward making technology more the servant and less the master.

There is plenty of work for everyone in responding to the predictions. It is clear that the public sector will have to exercise even more initiative in identifying and supporting candidates for office with commitment to better ways of educating for integrative, systemic thinking; a realistic perception of the critical role of science in ecological planning; higher priority on studies of foreign languages; and more creative, stimulating, and experiential methods of teaching. Initiatives from concerned citizens and business interests have a vital place in developing educational outcomes that can be competitive with the rest of the developing world and can continue to contribute to a better life for all.

(12)

EDUCATION FOR A DEMOCRACY: THE EVOLVING MESSAGE

I know no safe depository of the ultimate powers of the society but the people themselves; and if we think them not enlightened enough to exercise their control with a wholesome discretion, the remedy is not to take it from them but to enforce their discretion by education.

—Thomas Jefferson

Six months have passed since I began these observations on educational change and the importance of everybody's involvement in the process. During that time, the pace of change has quickened and the interactive scope of human affairs has been dramatically expanded—all against a backdrop of dynamic political developments and a highly energized electorate.

Now the fiercely contested presidential election campaign is finished, and we are positioned to examine further the familiar issue of relationships between school and society and the democratic system that determines their directions. There are those who would say that Jefferson foresaw the possibility of an electorate not enlightened enough to exercise their voting privilege with a "wholesome discretion." Casting a vote based solely on old habits and traditions or on single personal ideologies without concern for the fundamental national issues, their future directions, and the realities of the increasingly global, systemic interrelationships—such a vote calls for a review of Jefferson's wisdom. The remedy, he says, is to "enforce their discretion by education. This is the corrective of abuses of constitutional power" (Jefferson 1899, 161).

The predictive summary that I had planned to write for the final chapter of this book no longer seems practical. There can be no conclusions, no "last word and testament" in an uncertain, chaotic system. There are, however, a number of last-minute additions and observations that expand the understanding of the business of education and the reality of its place in everyone's thinking. An important feature of that reality is the fact that good intentions cannot be accomplished by old ways of thinking.

A serious look at the state of the world raises a question regarding the thought processes of decision makers in positions of overwhelming power and influence. Although leadership may bring advanced degrees and certifications to the positions of authority, the scope of their thinking may fail to go beyond a focus on present and personal political agenda. Years of traditional education are no guarantee of a mature intellect. Entrenched mentalities need to change, or institutions will continue to play the same old games and repeat the same old tunes. Schools and society have an opportunity and responsibility to change the tune.

The traditional "tune" of education was borrowed from mass-production methods that were so efficient in factories. However, we are learning that "direct experience" teaches at least as many lessons as books. If the school is repressive, children will distrust academic learning and avoid it in the future. No matter how important an idea, if it is presented in a boring way, children will turn away their attention. No matter what lofty ideas about democracy one reads in books or hears from teachers, if the local government is corrupt, cynicism is what will be learned (Csikszentmihalyi 1994, 272–76).

The following observations on education and society are both general and specific to the separate chapters. It is the nature of complex systems to have a quality of randomness at the same time that they may have a particular relationship to a focused issue. The integrative nature of the separate parts of the learning process is so profuse and crosshatched that a strictly sequential, orderly style is not possible; some ideas may appear in more than one context.

Recent months have been providing growing evidence that "education really is everybody's business." The current issue of *The Futurist*, a publication of the World Future Society, has a vigorous message on educational reform that is finding its way into the thinking of concerned citizens all over the world (Lundt 2004, 18–22). Lundt suggests that one of the most critical skills for coping with change is being able to learn, and that critics are faulting the education system for not helping to develop that skill. Further, he argues that funding for education is controlled by governments, and the content of education is controlled by education administrators, while learners have very little choice. The concerned public can make the choice to join in the leadership for new ways of making the student the customer.

In the same issue, Cynthia Wagner, managing editor of *The Futurist* and editor of *Futurist Update*, reports the 2004 meeting of the World Future Society and its focus on "improving our foresight, enhancing our intelligence, and developing partnerships with each other and with our rapidly advancing technologies." Her article on "Creating a More Intelligent Future" echoes arguments for many of the ideas proposed in this work (Wagner 2004, 48–52).

Schools and society together are designed to continue to create our democracy. The protection of citizens' right to speak freely on issues of public concern is guaranteed. As early as 1969, a landmark book by Postman and Weingartner reminded us of the responsibility of education to foster in students the understanding of their right to think and be heard. They said:

> One of the tenets of a democratic society is that men be allowed to think and express themselves freely on any subject, even to the point of speaking out against the idea of a democratic society. To the extent that our schools are instruments of such a society, they must develop in the young not only an awareness of this freedom but a will to exercise it and the intellectual power and perspective to do so effectively. (1)

Education, like everything else, is a living continuum. The past has a lot to do with defining the present, and the present has the potential to create the future. There are countless examples of efforts made in the past for educational change. "Understanding education backwards" can provide endless examples of serious efforts for change in the education community. I don't remember too much past attention in public media for raising the attention of the concerned public to participate in leadership for educational change. Now a survey of print media offers examples of persons and places that are "living education forwards" both within and outside the educational establishment. One major development in the matter of assessment of student achievement is beginning to be heard. Guilford College in Greensboro, North Carolina, reports that their Habits of Mind program's list of objectives includes an item on "learning the value of self-assessment, starting with the identification of strengths and then deciding upon next steps, moving away from focusing on deficiencies and honoring the knowledge and beliefs they bring to the learning process" (Borrego 2004, 1–2). This is encouraging evidence that the seminal work on the development of a process for student self-assessment of achievement is finding its way into enlightened educational practices (McTighe and Wiggins 1999). The trend toward self-assessment of achievement by students would be a welcome relief from the controversial standardized assessment practices of the No Child Left Behind federal program.

It is encouraging to realize that news media are reporting promising trends in selected educational centers, and the reading public is paying attention. A story that includes the educational belief system of a member of the Minneapolis School Board can point the thinking of concerned public in new directions:

> We now assume that competition improves schools. I am not convinced. . . . Schools will be more competitive if we begin with a vision of what our young people need and deserve, and only then focus on what will sell; build on our advantages—small schools, diversity, teachers adept at teaching diverse populations, the cultural opportunities of the city, magnet programs; learn from the appeal of charter schools—respect, individual attention, cultural competence, and hope. We must have greater flexibility in deployment of teachers; be relentlessly honest about our successes, shortfalls, and strategies for improvement; achieve stability and predictability. (Shapiro 2004, B5)

And from a publication of the Association for Supervision and Curriculum Development:

> Integrating 21st century skills into the school curriculum can help create a path toward higher achievement by empowering students to take more

control of their own learning. Learning in schools becomes even more relevant and invigorating for students who are always learning in their lives outside of school, using the latest technologies to communicate, collaborate, work, and learn. (Marizio 2004)

All change requires a creative leap forward; the creative factor in education lays the groundwork for activating the creative potential in students, but creative thinking is being evoked everywhere that people gather to solve problems and move society along to a better place—even in government! Steve Dahlberg (2004) called attention to the reminder in the 9/11 Commission Report that it is "crucial to find a way of routinizing, even bureaucratizing, the exercise of imagination," and reported that "Congress called hearings to discuss the intelligence community's 'failure of imagination' and the 'requirement for imagination and creativity' going forward." He suggests that "developing one's creativity and imagination is not an untested area. And it is not simply the realm of artists, Hollywood-types, and geniuses as was often implied in the Congressional testimony" (Dahlberg 2004, 1–2). When schools become more deliberate about the teaching of thinking processes for future citizens, it will come as no surprise that the intelligence community and democratic governments practice creative thinking in their dealing with national and world challenges.

The creativity factor has many dimensions and levels of application, from the identification and development of creative talent to teaching strategies for the practice of imaginative, creative thinking, to specific steps for solving problems creatively, to self-expression and the creative life and profit in the marketplace. Beyond the more familiar and practical attention to creativity is the deeper philosophical level of thought that advances the discipline of creativity to a higher level. Efiong Etuk (2002) has created a remarkable reading experience for educators and public alike. His *Great Insights into Human Creativity: Transforming the Way We Live, Work, Educate, Lead, and Relate* has a unique appeal both for individuals who are introspective about their own creativity and for the universal population of serious scholars and activists hoping to move humanity along to a higher plane.

It is becoming more obvious that old habits of thought are not adequate to the challenges of a new kind of world. Old thinking is said to be "too linear, analytic, static, rationalistic, and hierarchical. The proposed new way of thinking is more horizontal, holistic, dynamic, intuitive, and network-like" (Lombardo and Richter 2004, 277). There is good reason for that statement when it is followed by the reminder that "we would be lost without linear thinking and without analytic thought, logic and science would go out the window and life would be reduced to a chaotic blur." There is no denial of the importance of logical, analytical thought; the argument is for a better balance between holistic, systemic thinking and logical, analytical processing of information. The best of both worlds would provide the service of specialists in analytical, "left-brain" thinking for the promotion of balance with a broader, "right-brain," more futuristic vision in problem solving and decision making.

The need for new ways of thinking nationally and globally is not an invention of the twenty-first century. Who can forget the dramatic arrival on the scene of a book by a Soviet leader in 1987, *Perestroika: New Thinking for Our Country and the World* (Gorbachev 1987)? It was a most singular appeal for the people of the world to think. Much trouble could have been avoided if his appeal had been heard and responded to. The message is still valid in most places and institutions.

Education is the logical place for the development of new ways of thinking. Standardization of teaching and learning places limits on the potential of many students to discover their intellectual potential. Specialists in human potential like Win Wenger (1998) have been telling the population that most of us are smarter than we think and that schooling can practice strategies that accelerate learning and thinking for all students.

There is a growing list of writers who continue to tell the world about ways of understanding and practicing the art of thinking and being. The practice of mindfulness meditation (Kabat-Zinn 1994) can have a place in habits of thought. Mihaly Csikszentmihalyi (1993) has brought to our attention his thoughts for unlocking the hearts and minds of all learners with his description of the "Flow" theory. To top it off, there is Ken Wilbur's *A Theory of Everything: An Integral Vision for Business, Politics, Science, and Spirituality* (2000). The daunting task of education is to be alert to the changing tapestry of life beyond the institution and to provide guidance and support for the development of individual potential that continues to evolve during all of a lifetime of human satisfaction and service.

On the practical economic side of the education equation, the idea that business can exercise an influence on education is having increased attention. William Coplin (2004), professor of public affairs at Syracuse University, is telling business leaders that they should participate on advisory boards that influence curricula by developing a list of skills that they want in their employees, including work ethic, honesty, skills of teamwork, leadership, writing, oral communication, and problem solving, along with computer and research skills. Business leaders can then promote the skills in contacts they develop with students and professional education groups.

An addition to the effort for business's influencing of education is the reminder that creativity = capital and that creativity is the most renewable resource available to any profit-seeking organization. A note of warning was issued recently by Ronald Bosrock in his column for the Business Forum section of the *Minneapolis Star Tribune*. He suggested that "the world is catching up to traditional American world leadership not only in sports, but also in manufacturing, technology, engineering skills, and the quantity and quality of the education system that's essential for a winning economy and that the future of our economy will be directly connected to the quality of the students we produce" (2004, D3).

That consideration should be enough to jump-start the attention and action of the business community to take seriously the challenge of influencing required educational experiences and curricula.

Attention to the domain of business and capital is only part of a much grander system. Albert Einstein had a message that envisioned an inclusive world. He said it this way:

> A human being is part of the whole, called by us "universe," a part limited in time and space. He experiences himself, his thoughts and feelings, as something separated from the rest—a kind of delusion of his consciousness. This delusion is a prison for us, restricting us to our personal desires and to affection for a few persons nearest to us. Our task must be to free ourselves from this prison by widening our circle of compassion to embrace all living creatures and the whole of nature in its beauty. (Abdullah 1999, 9)

United States International University was one place where learning, accompanied by the presence of students from sixty different countries, had the effect of opening our doors of perception and widening the circle of our understanding and compassion (Dil 2004). When Viktor Frankl became acquainted with USIU, he said that he had found more hope in higher education at United States International University than anywhere else, and suggested that a Statue of Responsibility be built on the West Coast and that USIU would be the ideal spot to erect such a statue.

People of prominence in our world have not been idle in their initiatives for leadership in the transition to a global society. In September 1990, at a time of momentous international developments, the First International Dialogue on the Transition to a Global Society met at Landegg Academy in Switzerland. Officials and other people of prominence from around the world met for an exchange of global visionary thought and dialogue. They were joined by invitees who were practitioners of educational connections to global studies. I was privileged to be among that group. We listened to formal presentations and participated in the dialogue that followed. Members of different nationalities, cultures, races, and disciplines became unified in their concerns for "the way ahead." The report of the event includes the belief that, in so doing, the "human creative faculty is released, and the achievement of unity and integration becomes genuinely possible" (Bushrui, Ayman, and Laszlo 1993). Its members also made a detailed report to the United Nations' Conference on Environment and Development in Rio de Janeiro in 1992 for the Earth Summit.

The history of positive change in the world continues to remind us that it is the people or sometimes the single human—rather than the abstract institution—who initiates and implements positive change. There is every reason to deliver education in a way that discovers and cultivates intellectual talents for creative thinking and change agentry in behalf of a world in the grips of a major transition. For many years, the importance of creative expression has been focusing on children and youth. We are now recognizing the same need for self-expression among the senior members of society.

Again, it was E. Paul Torrance who led the way for attention to the concept of creative aging. Responding creatively to change is a talent much to be hoped for when change happens. Torrance believed that with the aging process "opportunities for leisure and non-work provide opportunities for growth, learning, enlightenment, and the chance to build a better world. Leisure is no longer a luxury but an essential of life, and it must be embraced with a positive attitude or it will become a burden" (Torrance 1995, 101). The good news is that many older people become free to be themselves and to be creative for the first time without the threat of job loss or ridicule from social traditionalists. Social programs and agencies have been offering opportunities for arts and crafts for seniors. Extending the involvement to include the study of creative leadership and its application to educational and other social and political change would create a new dimension for service to the independent privileges of a democracy.

We hear often about the educational concern regarding the differences between standardized achievement scores of minority students and white students. Torrance understood so well the importance of discovering special talents in *all* students and that rewarding them created a confidence in students for working at the development of other skills. His belief in the power of mentoring for discovering and supporting individual abilities in all students led to the publication of the book *Multicultural Mentoring of the Gifted and Talented* (Torrance, Goff, and Satterfield 1998). This work is a valuable resource for educators who are serious about closing the cultural achievement gap.

An additional Torrance publication of interest to the career-minded, young and old, is *The Manifesto: A Guide to Developing a Creative Career* (Torrance 2002). This is a book with sentimental response from Torrance colleagues because it was produced during the final years of his life, when the strength of his courage and commitment were so evident, and because his manifesto can be seen as a blueprint of his own creative life and legacy.

The academic discipline of creativity that Torrance presided over for fifty years has as its experiential introduction to the serious studies of creativity the long-established creative problem-solving process described earlier. Countless written and oral reports testify to the "whack on the side of the head" that was delivered when participants were introduced to an experience with creative problem solving. The freedom to think and create ideas independently, with no fear of rejection, plus thinking together with other imaginative minds turned on what was the greatest possible mental breakthrough. My first encounter with the process at the Creative Problem Solving Institute in Buffalo, New York, in the mid-1960s, was the beginning of a new intellectual energy and new expectations of my life and its possibilities. It was a powerful message that has never changed. The theme for the 2005 Institute, "The Future Beckons," says it all.

If there is one recommendation to be made to efforts for an education makeover, it would be to see to it that every teacher have a firsthand experience with the awakening of the creative spirit that comes with the practice of disciplined, creative problem solving. Understanding its value for oneself would transfer to the understanding of the importance of creative expression for all students. The precepts of progressive education offered in 1961 by L. Cremin (Torrance 1995, 56) would be well served:

- Individual differences among children must be recognized.
- We learn best by doing and by having a vital interest.
- Education is a continuous reconstruction of living experience that goes beyond the four walls of the classroom.
- The classroom should be a laboratory for democracy.
- Social goals, as well as laboratory goals, are important.
- A child must be taught to think critically rather than accept blindly.

If teachers and administrators and the centers of educational power agreed on the validity of those precepts, we could have more confidence that institutionalized learning would produce citizens who are ready to exercise the voting privileges of a democracy with reason and judgment based on respect for the system and for the common good.

Thinking is essentially a process of problem solving, and problem solving is the essence of creative leadership. Peter Senge tells us to "forget your old tired ideas about leadership. The most successful corporation of the 1990s will be something called a learning organization. As the world becomes more complex and dynamic, work must become more learningful" (1990, 3). This means that schools will also have to become learningful institutions. If they want to develop leadership for a global future, they will have to be sure that students are practiced in the arts of creative and critical thinking, that they are comfortable and effective systems thinkers, and that they have learned to share in a common vision and to work together to achieve it.

The mental conditioning that accompanies the disciplined practice of creative problem solving trains the mind for deferring judgment and taking the time for carefully considered thought. Deferring judgment avoids the trap of an immediate response to an issue that sets up a spontaneous, established position that will have to be defended to the bitter end. Effective leadership uses the knowledge of the world from books and computer data banks. But the wisdom of the world that takes the knowledge and applies it to the human condition is in the minds and hearts of enlightened thinkers everywhere.

There will be more wisdom in the complex interdependent affairs of the world if educational leadership can make the move to teach thinking. The expectation that people like Torrance had in the 1960s, when he predicted that schools would be placing an emphasis not only on learning but equally on quality thinking—that prediction had not yet come to pass in 1994, according to Joseph Hester (1994). He observed that "although thinking has been researched and recommended, the applications of these findings in textbooks, college teacher courses and classroom strategies is sadly lacking. On a large scale, the call for teaching-for-thinking has not been heard" (8). With current federal mandates, such as the No Child Left Behind Act, there is faint hope that there will be much more action in the near future unless public opinion makes itself heard.

A major leap forward on the issue of leadership has appeared on the scene recently in *The Leadership of Civilization Building* (Spady and Kirby 2002). It is a serious reminder that it is time for leadership to open those doors of perception that move our thinking beyond local affairs and beyond state and national affairs to embrace the entire civilized world. All levels of society would be included, but the old patterns of absolute nationalism and conflicted two-dimensional thinking would be transcended in attention to civilization building. The human mind is quite capable of such a level of complex thinking, but schools will have to provide the preparation and practice for its development. Educational institutions will probably need persuasion and support from a strong public voice.

There is no better model for the teaching of complex thinking than the global environment, with its constancy of change. There is something very real and compelling in the consideration of the beauty and mechanism of the real-world interactive system. The abstract data and

knowledge that informs us of the environmental realities cannot begin
to communicate the sensory response and depth of feeling that happens
when we are present in the real, magical, and mysterious world of nature. Environmental studies in schools at every level can give students
both intellectual and emotional understanding of the planet and its future. The planetary home of all of civilization depends upon the entire
intergenerational community for its preservation. The critical role of
schools in the protection of the Earth is a major part of a message *Nurturing Civilization Builders: Birthing the Best Schools in the World*
(Gilles and Kirby 2004). The nature and practical idealism in the book's
message for both educators and educationally concerned citizens is
made clear in the preface:

> Let's celebrate what it means to be human and share our own special
> gifts—visible and invisible, inner and outer—while uniting our vision for
> a more compassionate, sustainable and just way of life. The foundation for
> this vision is built on our hearts' deepest desires and the inherent worth
> of all life. As we, the nurturers of civilization builders, choose to co-create
> a new era of well being, we inspire hope, draw forth the best in each of us
> and become worthy leaders for our children and their future life on Earth
> and in space. (xvi)

Present social realities seem a poor match for the vision of hope and
well-being. Many social commentators and psychologists are reminding
us that

> Our modern, high-tech, fast-paced world is becoming increasingly fren-
> zied and fragmented. In a time when we possess more financial wealth,
> material goods, and technological conveniences than ever before, we suf-
> fer from chronic stress and anxiety, information and choice overload, a de-
> crease in perceived happiness, feelings of loss of control, deterioration in
> interpersonal trust and connectivity, and an epidemic of escalating de-
> pression. (Lombardo and Richter 2004, 257)

A balance between science and the humanities in society and in our
educational institutions is not an impossible achievement. In 2002, Ce-
cilia Yau created a comprehensive study, *Breakthroughs and Beyond:
Twentieth-Century Scientific Revolutions and Artistic Innovations*. It is

a revealing investigation of leading theorists, adventurers, independent thinkers, and experimenters of the world who have created new ideas and knowledge that provide breakthroughs in our understanding and expand our perceptions. Some are scientists who explore the depths of the scientific principles and structures of the universe; some are artists who "tear apart the illusion of a rational and orderly being and expose the contradictory, irrational and compulsive drives within human nature" (Yau 2002). Yau has provided a fascinating and scholarly book that celebrates the balance between scientific and humanistic creative contributions to our understanding of our world and our humanity.

Balance and the integration of differences are hallmarks of superior intellect. A classic example of that balance took place in a series of casual conversations at United States International University some years ago. Buckminster Fuller, renowned scientist, and Anwar Dil, renowned artist/philosopher, met a number of times when Fuller was a visiting professor on the campus of the university where Dil was a member of the faculty. Their unique dialogue was captured on tape and appeared serendipitously later in *Humans in Universe* (Fuller and Dil 1983). The exchange between Fuller and Dil, West and East, scientist and philosopher, is a revelation of the harmony that is fundamental to the open minds of specialists of differences and distinction.

We may not all be intellectual giants, but we are all thinkers. The habits of thought that are practiced and perpetuated in a lifetime determine our belief systems and our behaviors. If schools everywhere fail to exercise higher-order complex thinking processes throughout the curricula, the world will find it difficult to escape the recurring conflicts between people of cultural, political, and religious differences. Civilization can think its way out of the morass of the human dilemma, but the groundwork will have to be laid during the learning years, and it had better begin without delay.

Many are aware of the history of Vaclav Havel, who became president of Czechoslovakia in 1989. His story is told from a conversation—conducted by letter and tape recorder in 1986—with Karel Hvizdala, a Czech journalist living in West Germany. Havel's story is a record of both the tribulations and triumphs that are accompaniments to courageous efforts for reform that end up "disturbing the peace" (Hvizdala 1990).

It is not the intention of this writer to encourage educational activists to risk imprisonment for disturbing the peace of education-as-usual. It is intended simply as a wake-up call to advocates of educational change and enlightened educationists to join ranks in creative strategies for making a difference. Together, they can bring forward to centers of power and influence an argument for new ways of thinking for a new kind of world and the specific teaching of thinking processes that will help get human society to a better place now and in future time. Democracy deserves the best thinking possible.

APPENDIX A:
MIND MAP

Figure A.1. A Simple Example of Mind Mapping Based on the Operations Dimension of the Guilford Model of the Structure of the Intellect.

APPENDIX B:
BEYONDER SURVEY AND KEY

ARE YOU A BEYONDER?

The word "Beyonder" is not in the dictionary. The term was created by Dr. Torrance during his research when he recognized the need for a word to describe respondents to tests of creative thinking who "had so many notable creative achievements that they did not fit on the same scale as the other respondents." The survey is the result of a study that identified characteristics of a population of highly creative achievers in history and in the acquaintance of the researcher. They may be seen as the same characteristics that describe a style of leadership that is often undesignated and unrecognized. (The following is taken from E. P. Torrance, *Why Fly?* [Norwood, N.J.: Ablex, 1995]. Used with permission.)

BEYONDER CHECKLIST, BY E. PAUL TORRANCE

Please check the statements that usually describe your feelings. Be as honest and objective as possible.

1. I have experienced many ups and downs.
2. My behavior is difficult to predict.

3. My horoscope hardly ever predicts my behavior.
4. Even as a baby, I knew I was no ordinary person.
5. I feel that I have an important mission in life.
6. I usually go beyond the usual scope in trying to understand things.
7. I sometimes wonder why I have so much good luck.
8. I usually consider myself a giver rather than a taker.
9. I am not a well-rounded person; there are many rather ordinary things I cannot do
10. I will repay a debt even when I do not have to.
11. When I have failed, I have picked myself up and tried again.
12. I am honest even when it hurts.
13. I love all living creatures.
14. I try to use my energy constructively.
15. I may fail a hundred times, but I will not give up if I love it and believe in it.
16. I learn much from the experiences of others.
17. I like a challenge, even though I have to work hard.
18. I enjoy being with young children or working with them.
19. At times I have felt very alone.
20. I look forward to retirement as my "golden years."
21. There are few people who have loved their work as I have.
22. Few people in my field have had the courage that I have.
23. I believe that the most important mission in life is to give without end.
24. I have always had a high energy level.
25. My job is better than working for a living.
26. I have outbursts of levity occasionally.
27. When I am in doubt, I will often go ahead and try it.
28. My behavior is guided by a clear purpose.
29. I feel comfortable in being a minority of one.
30. Even as a child, I knew I was different.
31. I am usually a chance-taker.
32. It is fun to discover the reason behind things.
33. Problems or new ideas won't go away for me. They creep into my mind at odd times.
34. I find that I usually make a lot of mistakes in order to accomplish much.

35. Deep thinking is real fun—more fun than much of the social con-
     versation I get involved in.

TABLE FOR CONVERTING RAW SCORES TO PERCENTILE RANK ON THE BEYONDER CHECKLIST

Raw Scores	Frequency	Cum. Frequency	Percentile
1	0	0	0
2	1	1	1
3	0	1	1
4	0	1	1
5	0	1	1
6	1	2	1
7	1	2	2
8	3	5	2
9	2	7	3
10	7	14	6
11	8	22	9
12	14	36	15
13	8	44	19
14	27	72	31
15	21	93	40
16	20	118	48
17	17	129	55
18	20	149	64
19	14	163	70
20	12	175	76
21	14	189	81
22	14	203	87
23	4	208	89
24	10	218	94
25	5	222	95
26	4	226	97
27	3	228	98
28	1	230	99
29	2	232	100
30	0	232	100
31	0	232	100
32	0	232	100
33	0	232	100
34	0	232	100
35	0	232	100

Note: You obtain your score by counting the number of items checked. Determine your rank by using the scoring table and looking up your raw score to see what percentile rank it converts into. These data are based on the responses of superior adults. Certain items are more characteristic of Beyonders than a general sample of superior adults.

APPENDIX C:
STATEMENTS FROM STUDENTS

Excerpts from undergraduate student evaluations of the course on creative problem solving, entrepreneurship program, University of St. Thomas, Minneapolis, Minnesota.

- Immensely practical material.
- I feel a little more open—a little more willing to take some chances that I might not have before.
- We did activities that we never would have done out of class to become more creative.
- I found this course to be very stimulating in relation to creativity and creative thinking.
- It made me "rediscover" the potential I have myself and the potential of others
- I realized that in order to enjoy the world and get the most out of it, I have to keep on my toes but also take the time to learn, discover, and grow.
- I found the course to be a real acceptance experience. Many of the ideas that I have had for a long time were thought to be absurd or out of the ordinary. By the same token, I also found that during my experience at St. Thomas and this class that discipline is as much a tool as is creativity. As for negative aspects of this class, I quite

honestly did not find any. All matters were clear. Assignments were clear and to the point. And your excitement and concern for the topics was quite enlightening.

- The course has helped me be more aware of my own personal objectives in life; it relates to them and I can use many of the techniques we learned in class.
- At first I was hesitant about the class being in a business major. But as I started to get more into it, it does relate to all fields, even nursing!
- As a future parent (some day) I'm aware of the faults in our school system, and hope I can compensate for them with my children in the home, especially "wild and crazy" brainstorming.
- One concern or hope I have is that others can somehow learn and develop in ways I have from this class. I wish you the best of luck in expanding and reaching more students!
- Different. I've never had a class in any vicinity of the directions we went while in the classroom.
- The topic was different but the means of the teaching the material was also different. Many times, it would have been much easier for the teacher and the students to fall back into the familiar confines of academia. We never went back into the rut. By the end of the course, that fact became very refreshing.
- The enthusiasm of the students increased steadily as the year went on.
- This entrepreneurial creative problem-solving course was excellent in providing the opportunity for individual thinking. It provided an awareness of each individual's capacity to come up with ideas and to stand by their value.
- Many things brought up in this course are practical and can be used for other areas
- I just want to inform the school that this is the best course I have taken at St. Thomas. It allowed a lot of creative thoughts to be processed. I would consider this the best course at St. Thomas.
- I have enjoyed BA 250 very much and have found the class to be very stimulating for thinking creatively. I would recommend this class for all business majors to stimulate thinking yet learn a lot about business. I loved it! It really showed that there is a lot of opportunity.

- I enjoyed this class and was present about every day. My curiosity was prevalent not to miss class. I learned things from this course that I will carry with me and utilize for a long time. This is an exceptional class and I would recommend it to everyone.
- An outstanding professor—really learned a lot. It opened my mind a lot.
- The class was stimulating and taught me more than I've learned in a lot of other classes, made me believe in myself!
- I have learned a lot of valuable information in this course. She was very informed in the course and taught a lot of current information.
- This is by far the best course I've taken in three years at C.S.T. Very relevant to much of today's business ideas. I'd recommend this class to any one, business or not. I wouldn't have a thing changed!!
- Without doubt, this class has been the best I've ever taken whilst here at Thomas. I've learned and retained more in this class than any other. You are a fine facilitator! Bravo!! I have never recommended any class as often or as highly as I have recommended yours. Thank you for your time and ideas. This is the best $800.00 that I've ever spent.
- I would like to take the course again to pick up everything I missed the first time. I think the course would continue to teach if you took it 10 times.
- This opened a whole new area for me—Dr. Bleedorn so carefully presents information that novices don't get lost, yet entices stimulating discussions. She also keeps track of where we're going and how long we can stay there.
- Dr. Bleedorn is concerned and enthusiastic, supportive of students, leads with encouragement—terrific! She makes us look good!
- The production of creative thought came very creatively—in ways I didn't expect.

FALL SEMESTER

- The course has opened my mind to look at problems and opportunities in a much broader view.

- I now can see various ways to approach situations with much more depth.
- The concepts of the course have been put to use in and out of the classroom. Everyday problems have been turned into opportunities—the topics studied open up a person's mind to look beyond the obvious.
- This course was a great help to me. It brought out my creativity that I had never thought of before.
- There was good variety in the class. The readings and text were very appropriate
- The final project was great—The most valuable aspect of this course has been the realization that the creative process can be taught and practiced. I was always under the impression that one either was or was not creative, and that there wasn't much one could do about the state of their ability to be creative.
- Learning about the various procedures for problem identification and problem solving helped out a lot, as I now can use those procedures to a degree with many problems I encounter.
- I would highly recommend this course to anyone interested in broadening their ability to be open minded.
- The value of learning to suspend judgment has already been apparent in my own life, and it is something I will continue to use.
- I found the course very valuable because it helped me to become more aware of my thought process and how to nurture an idea from start to finish.
- Besides increasing my awareness, this course is responsible for helping me to make changes in my life, such as I now carry an "Idea Trap" around with me. I've found the value of this pays off in helping preserve those delicate insights which every person has.
- The problem solving process, as laid out in class, showed me how, in the future, if I am having trouble deciding how to do something, following that process would be extremely helpful—The final project helped tie down everything we learned throughout the semester.

One student felt so strongly about this course that he wrote a letter to the Department Chair, Small Business, University of St. Thomas, Minneapolis, Minnesota. The following is excerpted from his letter.

I am a student currently enrolled at the College of St. Thomas majoring in Business. Just recently, I have declared Entrepreneurship as my main focus. One of the courses in my major which I have found to be extremely instrumental in my studies is Entrepreneurial Creative Thinking and Problem Solving instructed by Berenice D. Bleedorn, Ph.D.

Through this course, I have learned that entrepreneurs and intrapreneurs are becoming widely accepted in the business community. For so long I believed that one studied for a particular job, got a degree in that field, interviewed and were hired, and then quietly "performed the duties, as assigned." I have come to realize, through this class, that talented intrapreneurs are now being nurtured in the business place, and more and more entrepreneurs are succeeding. This class offers an arena for expanding your mind to greater creativity and has supported me in overcoming many obstacles that might have stopped me in the past.

The class, itself, may have offered all of these things; but, for me, the catalyst that really made it work was Dr. Bleedorn. I expect college instructors to be well-qualified, however, she not only has the background in the subject, she also stays current with what is happening in the world of entrepreneurs. She has brought interesting guests, movies, publications and assignments to the class.

With these things in mind, I am writing to suggest that this course be required for all students pursuing a degree in Business. It was in this environment that I learned to cultivate my creativity, believe in myself, and pursue some of my own dreams. Entrepreneurial Creative Thinking and Problem Solving would assist any Business major, regardless of their focus.

I appreciate any consideration you give to this request. I know that curriculum does not change with one letter, but I felt that it was important enough to speak out.

REFERENCES

Abdullah, S. 1999. *Creating a world that works for all*. San Francisco, CA: Barrett Koehler.

Arlington Institute. *Futuredition 6, 22, 6*.

Beuys, J. 1998. Creativity = Capital. Joseph Beuys Multiples Exhibit, Walker Art Center, Minneapolis, Minn..

Bleedorn, B. 1988. *Creative leadership for a global future: Studies and speculations*. New York: Peter Lang.

———. 1996. Business Forum: For lessons in teamwork try listening to some jazz. *Minneapolis Star Tribune*, November 11.

———. 1998. *The creativity force in business, education, and beyond: An urgent message*. Lakeville, Minn.: Galde Press.

———. 2003. *An education track for creativity and other quality thinking processes*. Lanham, Md.: Scarecrow Education Press.

Bohm, D. 1998. On creativity. In *On Creativity*, edited by L. Nichol, 1–26. London: Routledge.

Borrego, M. 2004. *Guilford College Habits of Mind Bulletin*. Greensboro, N.C.

Bosrock, R. 2004. Quit kidding around with schools. *Minneapolis Star Tribune*, August 30, D3.

Botkin, J., M. Elmandjra, and M. Malitza. 1979. *No limits to learning: A report to the Club of Rome*. New York: Pergamon Press.

Budhwami, N. 2003. A call to action. *LINK* (University of Minnesota): 21.

Burns, J. 1978. *Leadership*. New York: Harper & Row.

Bushrui, S., I. Ayman, and E. Laszlo. 1993. *Transition to a global society*. Wienacht, Switzerland: Landegg Academy.

Buzan, T., and B. Buzan. 1993. *The mind map book: How to use radiant thinking to maximize your brain's untapped potential*. New York: Penguin Books.

Callahan, D. 2004. *The cheating culture: Why more Americans are doing wrong to get ahead*. New York: Harcourt.

Caplan, W. 2004. Businesses need to dive into education. *Syracuse University*, September 19.

Cleveland, H. 1980. Learning the art of leadership. *Twin Cities Magazine*, 27–34.

———. 1984. Leaders as "first birds off the telephone wire." *Leading Edge* (November 5): 2.

———. 1993. *Birth of a new world: An operating manual for international leadership*. San Francisco, Calif.: Jossey-Bass.

Coates, J. 2004. Where science is headed. *Journal of the Washington Academy of Sciences* 89 (no. 3–4, Winter): 16–22.

Coplin, W. 2004. Businesses need to dive into education. *Syracuse University* (September).

Csikszentmihalyi, M. 1994. Educating for a good society. *The evolving self*. New York: Harper Collins.

Dahlberg, S. 2004. *Creativity by choice, not by chance*. Retrieved from www.creativeeducationfoundation.org.

Didsbury, H. 2004. *Thinking creatively in turbulent times*. Bethesda, Md.: World Future Society.

Dil, A. 2004. Intercultural education: *Reminiscences of United States International University*. San Diego, Calif.: Takshila Research University.

Dimnet, E. 1928. *The art of thinking*. New York: Simon & Schuster.

Drucker, P. 1989. How schools must change. *Psychology Today* (May).

Dubos, R. 1968. *So human an animal*. New York: Charles Scribner's Sons.

Earth Charter. 2004. Values and principles for a sustainable future. Promotion Literature San Jose, Costa Rica: Earth Charter International Secretariat, c/o University for Peace. Retrieved from www.earthcharter.org.

Etuk, E. 2002. *Great insights on human creativity: Transforming the way we live, work, educate, lead, and relate*. Blacksburg, Va.: Unity Scholars.

Fallows, J., and V. Ganesshananthan. 2004. The big picture. *Atlantic Monthly* (October): 126.

Fantini, M., and G. Weinstein. 1969. *Toward a contact curriculum*. New York: Anti-Defamation League of B'nai B'rith.

Florida, R. 2002. *The rise of the creative class*. New York: Basic Books.

Fryer, M. 1996. *Creative teaching and learning*. London: Paul Chapman.

Fuller, B., and A. Dil.1983. *Humans in universe*. New York: Mouton.

Gardner, H. 1986. *The mind's new science*. New York: Basic Books.

———. 1993. *Creating minds*. New York: Basic Books.

Gelb, M. 1995. *Thinking for a change: Discovering the power to create, communicate, and lead*. New York: Harmony Books.

———. 1998. *How to think like Leonardo da Vinci*. New York: Delacorte Press.

Gilles, B., and R. Kirby. 2004. *Nurturing civilization builders: Birthing the best schools in the world*. Edmonds, Wash.: Oak Forest Press.

Gorbachev, M. 1997. *Perestroika: New thinking for us and for the world*. New York: Harper & Row.

Gowan, J. 1968. *Creativity: Its educational implications*. New York: McGraw Hill.

Grossman, S. 1988. *Innovation, Inc.: Unlocking creativity in the workplace*. Plano, Tex.: Wordware.

Gruchow, P. 2003. New standards leave no room for critical thinking. *Minneapolis Star Tribune*, November 25, D2.

Guilford, J. 1977. *Way beyond the IQ: Guide to improving intelligence and creativity*. Buffalo, N.Y.: Creative Education Foundation.

Harman, W. 1988. *Global mind change*. Indianapolis, Ind.: Knowledge Systems.

Harman, W., and J. Hormann. 1990. *Creative work: The constructive role of business in a transforming society*. Indianapolis, Ind.: Knowledge Systems.

Hassel, C., and G. Spangler. 2004. Science isn't the only way to truth. *Minneapolis Star Tribune*, August 1, A5.

Hester, J. 1994. *Teaching for thinking: A program for school improvement through teaching critical thinking across the curriculum*. Durham, N.C.: Carolina Academic Press.

Houston, J. 1992. The psychenaut program: An exploration into some human potentials. In *Source book for creative problem solving*, edited by S. Parnes. Buffalo, N.Y.: Creative Education Foundation Press.

Hvizdala, K. 1990. *Vaclav Havel: Disturbing the peace*. New York: Alfred Knopf.

Isaksen, S., and D. Treffinger. 2004. Celebrating 50 years of reflective practice: Versions of Creative Problem Solving. *Journal of Creative Behavior* 38 (no. 2): 75–101.

Jaccaci, A. 2000. *General periodicity: Nature's creative dynamics*. Scarborough, Me.: Fiddlehead.

Jamison, K. R. 2004. *Exuberance: The passion for life*. New York: Alfred A. Knopf.

Jedynak, G. 2005. Science, education, and self-assessment. Unpublished paper.

Jefferson, T. 1899. Letters to William Jarvis, September, 1820. *Writings of Thomas Jefferson* 10:161.

Kabat-Zinn, J. 1994. *Wherever you go, there you are: Mindfulness meditation in everyday life*. New York: Hyperion.

Kaufman, W. 1970. On dualistic thinking. *University: A Princeton Quarterly* 44 (Spring): 3–6.

Kelley, K. 1988. *The home planet*. Reading, Mass.: Addison-Wesley.

Lombardo, T., and J. Richter. 2004. A new conceptual framework of thinking. *Thinking creatively in turbulent times*, edited by H. Didsbury. Bethesda, Md.: World Future Society Press.

Lott, A., and C. Schmidt. 2004. *Creating world citizens through global classrooms: A grant proposal for Model United Nations*. Minneapolis: United Nations Association of Minnesota.

Lundt, J. 2004. Learning for ourselves: A new paradigm for education. Learning should be taken out of the hands of antiquated school systems and put in the hands of the learners. *Futurist* (November–December): 18–22.

MacKinnon, D. 1978. *In search of human effectiveness: Identifying and developing creativity*. Buffalo, N.Y.: Bearly.

Maritzio, A. 2002. *The future is now: Learning in the 21st century*. Alexandria, Va.: Association for Supervision and Curriculum Development.

McTighe, J., and G. Wiggins. 1999. *Understanding by design workbook*. Alexandria, Va.: Association for Supervision and Curriculum Development.

Mearns, H. 1958. *Creative power*. New York: Dover.

Meltz, B. 2004. Evolving future consciousness through the pursuit of virtue. *Minneapolis Star Tribune*, February 8, E8. (Reprint from the *Boston Globe*).

Mestenhauser, J., and B. Ellingboe. 1998. *Reforming the higher education curriculum: Internationalizing the campus*. Phoenix, Ariz.: Oryx Press.

Millar, G. 1995. *E. Paul Torrance: The creativity man*. Norwood, N.J.: Ablex.

———. 2004 *The making of a Beyonder: Ways to nurture your creative achievement and spirit*. Bensenville, Ill.: Scholastic Testing Service.

Miller, J. 2001. Fostering a learning and creative organizational climate. *Minneapolis Star Tribune*, April 25, B9.

Mische, P. 2004. Letter to Global Education Associates. *Breakthrough News* (July–September).

Muller, P. 2003. The light at the end of the tunnel. in Bleedorn, B. *An education track for creativity and other quality thinking processes*. Lanham, MD: Scarecrow Education Press.

———. 2002. *Tomorrow is a new ball game: Visions of the future*. Pretoria, South Australia: LAPA.

Myers, I. 1980. *Myers-Briggs types indicators inventories*. Palo Alto, Calif.: Consulting Psychologist Press.

National Research Center on the Gifted and Talented Report. 2002. *E. Paul Torrance: His life, accomplishments, and legacy*. Storrs, Conn.: NRCG/T.

Noller, R., S. Parnes, and A. Biondi. 1976. *Creative action book*. New York: Charles Scribner's Sons.

Osborn, A. 1953. *Applied imagination*. New York: Charles Scribner's Sons.

Parnes, S. 1992a. *Visionizing*. Buffalo, N.Y.: Creative Education Press.

———, ed. 1992b. *Source book for creative problem solving*. Buffalo, N.Y.: Creative Education Press.

Pinchot, G., and R. Pellman. 1999. *Intrapreneuring in action: A handbook for business innovation*. San Francisco, Calif.: Berrett-Koehler.

Pitcher, G. 1961. The importance of being human. *Harvard Business Review* (January–February): 48.

Poindexter, E. 2004. Bleedorn, B. Creative leadership in a prison? Why not? *FOCUS: Newsletter of the American Creativity Association*, 16 (no. 1, January–February): 3.

Postman, N., and C. Weingartner. 1969. *Teaching is a subversive activity*. New York: Delacorte Press.

Putnam, R. 2000. *Bowling alone: The collapse and revival of American community*. New York: Simon & Schuster.

Ray, P., and S. Anderson. 2000. *The cultural creatives: How 50 million people are changing the world*. New York: Random House.

Richards, M. 1964. *Centering in pottery, poetry, and person*. Middletown, Conn.: Wesleyan University Press.

Ruggiero, V. 1988. *The art of thinking: A guide to critical and creative thought*. New York: Harper & Row.

Russell, P. 1992. *The creative manager: Finding inner vision and wisdom in uncertain times*. San Francisco, Calif.: Jossey-Bass.

Sachdev, R. 2004. *Imagination is everything*, pp. 1-2. Tech Central Station: Where free markets meet technology.

Schmidt, W. 1994. A framework for learning with DISC. *Carlson Learning Company Journal*. Minneapolis, Minn.: Learning Organization.

Schmitt, W. 2004. *Pavek Museum of Broadcasting Newsletter* 15 (August): 3.

Schumacher, E. 1973. *Small is beautiful*. New York: Harper and Row.

Scott, S., M. Brennecke, and K. Engelsen. 2003. *Spiral dynamics: The eight levels of human consciousness*. Instructional Chart.

Senge, P. 1990. *The fifth discipline: The art and practice of the learning organization*. New York: Doubleday.

Shapiro, R. 2004. Candidates discuss ways to attract students. *Minneapolis Star Tribune*, October 18, B5.

Sölle, D. 1995. *Creative disobedience*. Cleveland, Ohio: Pilgrim Press.

Spady, R., and R. Kirby. 2002. *The leadership of civilization building: Administrative and civilization theory, symbolic dialogue, and citizen skills for the 21st century*. Seattle, Wash.: Forum Foundation.

Sternberg, R. 1988. *The nature of creativity: Contemporary psychological perspectives*. Cambridge: Cambridge University Press.

———. 2003. "Three Rs . . . Reasoning, Resilience, and Responsibility." APA Annual Convention.

Swartz, R., and S. Parks. 1994. *Infusing the teaching of critical and creative thinking into content instruction: A lesson design handbook for the elementary grades*. Pacific Grove, Calif.: Critical Thinking Press and Software.

Teilhard de Chardin, P. 1961. *Hymn of the universe*. New York: Harper & Row.

———. 1966. *Phenomenon of man*. New York: Harper & Row.

Torrance, E. P. 1965. *Constructive behavior: Stress, personality, and mental health*. Belmont, Calif.: Wadsworth Publishing.

———. 1967. *Understanding the fourth grade slump in creative learning: Report of cooperative research project 994*. Washington, D.C.: U.S. Office of Education.

———. 1980. *Torrance Tests of Creative Thinking*. Bensenville, Ill.: Scholastic Testing Service.

———. 1987. *Save tomorrow for the children*. Buffalo, N.Y.: Bearly.

———. 1995. *Why fly? A philosophy of creativity*. Norwood, N.J.: Ablex.

———. 2002. *The manifesto: A guide to developing a creative career*. Westport, Conn.: Ablex.

Torrance, E. P., K. Goff, and N. Satterfield. 1998. *Multicultural mentoring of the gifted and talented*. Waco, Tex.: Prufrock Press.

Torrance, E. P., and H. Safter. 1990. *The incubation model of teaching: Getting beyond the aha!* Buffalo, N.Y.: Bearly.

———. 1999. *Making the creative leap beyond*. Buffalo, N.Y.: Creative Education Foundation Press.

Tucker, R. 1977. Personality and potential leadership. *Political Science Quarterly* 92 (no. 3): 383–93.

United Nations Association of the United States of America. 2004. *Helping the United States help the world*. New York: UNA-USA.

Wagner, C. 2004. Creating a more intelligent future. *Futurist* (November–December): 48–52.

Wenger, W. 1994. *Discovering the obvious*. Gaithersburg, Md.: Win Wenger.

Wiggins, G. 1998. *Educative assessment: Designing assessments to inform and improve student performance.* San Francisco, Calif.: Jossey-Bass.

Wilbur, K. 2000. *A theory of everything: An integral vision for business, politics, science, and spirituality.* Boston, Mass.: Shambhala.

World Future Society. 2004. The art of foresight: Preparing for a changing world: A special report from the World Future Society. *Futurist* (May–June): 31–36.

Yau, C. 2002. *Breakthrough and beyond: Twentieth-century scientific revolution and artistic innovation.* St. Catherine's, Ont.: Lincoln Graphics Press.

Zuckerman, M. 2003. A hard look at what works. *U. S. News and World Report* (November 24): 84–85.

INDEX

ABOUT THE AUTHOR

Berenice Bleedorn is an educational entrepreneur who initiated and taught courses in creative studies and futures studies for more than thirty years in education and business departments of various universities before her retirement. She has conducted seminars and workshops for a cross-section of educational and community organizations locally, nationally, and internationally. Dr. Bleedorn has been a colleague of the Creative Education Foundation in Buffalo, New York, for thirty-five years and has been honored with both their Service Commitment and Distinguished Leader awards. She developed and directed the Institute for Creative Studies at the University of St. Thomas and has served in the Minnesota State Department of Education and as a member of the board of directors of United Nations Minnesota. Her B.S. in education and M.A. in educational psychology are from the University of Minnesota. Her doctorate in leadership and human behavior is from United States International University in San Diego.

Dr. Bleedorn was admitted to the Creative Problem Solving Institute Hall of Fame in a ceremony at the 2005 Annual Institute at the University of St. Thomas, St. Paul, Minnesota.

Dr. Bleedorn has said it succinctly in so many ways. Education in the 21st century is truly everybody's business. Parents, students, teachers, business, and organizations of all kinds must provide leadership collaboratively in creative, imaginative, and innovative ways for the continuous improvement of our educational systems at all levels. Her book is a basic argument for the fundamental need to educate students who can both think and solve problems they have not encountered before. —Frank Maraviglia, president, Creativity Unlimited.

Dr. Bleedorn has assembled a wealth of knowledge and advice for present-day educators that encapsulates what is needed in a world that is full of complexity and challenge for today's students. I would love to see every teacher and would-be teacher read and apply the contents of her book. —Doris J. Shallcross, Ed. D., professor emerita, University of Massachusetts/Amherst

I fully agree that education is everybody's business and congratulate Berenice Bleedorn on her valuable and meticulous work. I admire her continual effort and involvement with new ways of educating. Her ideas are reminders of some of my favorite philosophers and educational authorities. I especially appreciate her views on the nature and purpose of education and her perspective on the human development values rather than the present focus on the material side of life. —Angel C. Sanhueze, CEO CPS International Chile; past CEO of Kagan S.A. and other business organizations.

Education Is Everybody's Business: Valuing Creativity is a must read for all enlightened school administrators and concerned citizens. She advocates schooling that goes beyond the accumulation of facts to challenging the mind and stimulating the spirit using creative teaching as a vehicle. —Garnet W. Millar, Ph.D., education consultant, Edmonton, Alberta, and author of *E. Paul Torrance: The Creativity Man* and *The Making of A Beyonder.*

This is clearly Berenice Bleedorn's most important book on education-insightful and written with a sense of urgency; the result of a life time of reflection and advocacy. A "must read" for politicians, administrators and educators. —Piet Muller, M.A., Ph.D. Chairman, Dr. P.J. Muller & Associates, Pretoria, South Africa.

Bee Bleedorn's purpose—indeed, mission—is clear: to continue to arouse to action dormant sensitivities about the current state of education and the world. She brings to this task years of experience, talent, and passion. Her call is to everyone, not simply professional educators. When she declares that "Educational entrepreneurs are desperately needed both inside and outside of the establishment," everybody should heed her message, since every person; has a stake in the enterprise. Those of us working in museums and in the informal or "free-choice" learning sector particularly should take note since we are well positioned to implement much of what Bee advocates—the fostering of creative problem-solving and other higher-level thought processes, of global understanding, environmental stewardship, and integrative experiences. It is everybody's business to join ranks in creative strategies for making a difference. —Al DeSena, Ph.D., founding director of Exploration Place, Wichita, KS and The Carnegie Science Center, Pittsburgh, PA.

Dr. Bleedorn's book continues to expand upon her call to society for a future which embraces creative and enlightened education. The potential of human creativity is the greatest asset possessed by our world civilization. Effectively highlighting the present state of creative education, Dr. Bleedorn makes a strong case for well-orchestrated change. This is a compelling read for anyone interested in understanding human creativity and creative education. —Christina Coyle, M.A., President, Prizm Solutions, Amherst, NY.

Dr. Bee Bleedorn has written a call for the reinvention of education worldwide. Her visionary book has a wonderful integrity in that she is what she says totally. Hers is the archetypal story of the emergence of a global educator from her start as the teacher in a one-room schoolhouse in rural Minnesota to the leadership of educational entrepreneurs who are mentoring learners through the most important creative transformation in human evolutionary history. Here, at last, is the call and the guide to begin to teach and to learn about thinking about thinking. She makes us wonder where we have been all these eons. —August T. Jaccaci, Author of *General Periodicity: Nature's Creative Dynamics.*

Dr. Bleedorn has a unique capacity to cut to the chase in educational issues. In a keen blend of wit and wisdom, she brings us to the essence of what it takes to turn the tides to strengthen enlightened and effective democracy. The book is for everyone interested in furthering our democratic heritage. —Marilyn Fiedler, education consultant

Bee has been a leader in the movement to make the teaching of critical and creative thinking and creative problem solving a component of k–12 and college curricula and part of everyone's education. Through practice in thinking skills students can make many connections between formal schooling and everyday living. Her latest, *Education Is*

Everybody's Business could and should be the catalyst of educational transformation: validating the need for basic skills while honoring the great power of humans for higher-order thinking to analyze, synthesize, and evaluate in order to manage the challenges of today's world. —Louise Loomis, director of the New England Cognitive Center, assistant professor of Philosophy, University of Hartford.

Professor Bleedorn powerfully demonstrates the urgent need for a global rethinking of the concept, purpose, and practice of education . . . *Education is Everybody's Business: Valuing Creativity* is two things in one: A new, more adequate, more humane view of education; and a rallying call to all of us to join forces to implement view and, once again, to regain the joy of higher-order thinking and the fulfillment of democratic citizenry. —Efiong Etuk, Ph.D., founding director African Communities for Creativity and Innovation, author of *Great Insights on Human Creativity: Transforming the Way We Live, Work, Educate, Lead, and Relate.*

Bleedorn is relentless in her insistence that the need for good citizenship and leadership in dealing effectively with current world problems requires critical and creative thinking skills. If more bulldogs like Bleedorn would insist upon such educational imperatives, perhaps "thinking outside the box" might become more than a cliché in words but also a cliché in practice! —Coleen Rowley, retired FBI agent

A breath of fresh air runs throughout this book! Dr. Bleedorn has undertaken to get us thinking about the real world of children, education, and the broader context in which we vest hope in education to make this world a better place. She tells us what this will be like in a way that leads us in the direction of significant applications in the classroom and in the school that can make all students better thinkers. My own work on infusing critical and creative thinking into content instruction K–12 bears this out. We want students to learn how to make sure that their goals are worthwhile and how to exercise the wonderful creative abilities we all have stored up in our minds. Good education can do all that, and Dr. Bleedorn's book can't fail to stir us to move with great strides in that direction. —Robert Swartz, professor emeritus, University of Massachusetts at Boston and director of the National Center for Teaching Thinking, USA.

Bleedorn has done it. With insight and rigor she has developed a lasting and compelling argument for rethinking our approach to education. A special truth emerges about the kind of inspired leadership and creative thinking that is necessary to transform our institutions. —Michael Morrison, dean, University of Toyota, CA